ONE-POT COOKING

ONE-POT COOKING

A FABULOUS COLLECTION OF OVER 120 RECIPES FOR DELICIOUS DISHES
COOKED IN JUST ONE POT, SHOWN IN 450 STEP-BY-STEP PHOTOGRAPHS

INCLUDES OVEN AND STOVE-TOP ROASTS, PAELLAS, STEWS,
CURRIES, CASSEROLES, STIR-FRIES, SOUPS AND TAGINES

JENNI FLEETWOOD

HERMES
HOUSE

This edition is published by Hermes House, an imprint of Anness Publishing Ltd, Hermes House, 88–89 Blackfriars Road, London SE1 8HA; tel. 020 7401 2077; fax 020 7633 9499

www.hermeshouse.com; www.annesspublishing.com

If you like the images in this book and would like to investigate using them for publishing, promotions or advertising, please visit our website www.practicalpictures.com for more information.

Publisher: Joanna Lorenz
Managing Editor: Linda Fraser
Project Editor: Jennifer Schofield
Recipes by: Alex Barker, Michelle Berriedale-Johnson, Kit Chan, Jacqueline Clarke, Matthew Drennan, Sarah Edmonds, Joanna Farrow, Brian Glover, Nicola Graimes, Christine Ingram, Lucy Knox, Lesley Mackley, Sally Mansfield, Sallie Morris, Jennie Shapter, Anne Sheasby, Steven Wheeler, Kate Whiteman and Jeni Wright
Photographers: James Duncan, Ian Garlick, Michelle Garrett, Amanda Heywood, David Jordan, Dave King, William Lingwood, Patrick McLeavey, Thomas Odulate, Craig Robertson and Sam Stowell
Designer: Nigel Partridge
Editorial Reader: Richard McGinlay
Production Controller: Bessie Bai

Main front cover image shows Chicken Casserole with Winter Vegetables – for recipe, see page 70.

ETHICAL TRADING POLICY

At Anness Publishing we believe that business should be conducted in an ethical and ecologically sustainable way, with respect for the environment and a proper regard to the replacement of the natural resources we employ.
As a publisher, we use a lot of wood pulp in high-quality paper for printing, and that wood commonly comes from spruce trees. We are therefore currently growing more than 750,000 trees in three Scottish forest plantations. The forests we manage contain more than 3.5 times the number of trees employed each year in making paper for the books we manufacture.
Because of this ongoing ecological investment programme, you, as our customer, can have the pleasure and reassurance of knowing that a tree is being cultivated on your behalf to naturally replace the materials used to make the book you are holding.
For further information about this scheme, go to www.annesspublishing.com/trees

A CIP catalogue record for this book is available from the British Library.

Previously published as *One Pot*

PUBLISHER'S NOTE

Although the advice and information in this book are believed to be accurate and true at the time of going to press, neither the authors nor the publisher can accept any legal responsibility or liability for any errors or omissions that may have been made nor for any inaccuracies nor for any loss, harm or injury that comes about from following instructions or advice in this book.

NOTES

Bracketed terms are intended for American readers.
For all recipes, quantities are given in both metric and imperial measures and, where appropriate, in standard cups and spoons. Follow one set of measures, but not a mixture, because they are not interchangeable.
Standard spoon and cup measures are level. 1 tsp = 5ml, 1 tbsp = 15ml, 1 cup = 250ml/8fl oz.
Australian standard tablespoons are 20ml. Australian readers should use 3 tsp in place of 1 tbsp for measuring small quantities.
American pints are 16fl oz/2 cups. American readers should use 20fl oz/2.5 cups in place of 1 pint when measuring liquids.
Electric oven temperatures in this book are for conventional ovens. When using a fan oven, the temperature will probably need to be reduced by about 10–20°C/20–40°F. Since ovens vary, you should check with your manufacturer's instruction book for guidance.
Medium (US large) eggs are used unless otherwise stated.

CONTENTS

Introduction   **6**

One-pot Equipment   8

One-pot Cooking Techniques   10

One-pot recipes

Soups   12

Meat and Game Main Meals   30

Chicken and Poultry Main Meals   68

Fish and Shellfish Main Meals   88

Vegetarian Main Meals and Pasta   108

Side Dishes   134

Index   **158**

INTRODUCTION

What do spicy stir-fries, nourishing soups, delectable stews, robust roasts, and creamy risottos have in common? They are all one-pot dishes, easy to prepare, a pleasure to serve and the perfect choice for family and friends.

Elaborate dinner parties are a rarity these days. On the menu instead are simple dishes prepared with the minimum of fuss but with maximum flavour. Even celebrity chefs have turned their backs on fiddly food, preferring instead to take a second look at old favourites like Irish Stew, Spicy Venison Casserole and Cassoulet. Coq au Vin has also made a come-back, and it is gaining new converts among a generation that has never tasted that delicious combination of chicken, red wine, bacon and shallots.

Cooking in a single pot is wonderfully liberating. All that is needed is a bit of leisurely preparation, and then you can relax, secure in the knowledge that there will be no last-minute sauces to make or tricky toppings to produce. Serving a selection of side dishes is largely unnecessary, especially when the recipe includes vegetables, so you have the perfect excuse for sparing yourself the anxiety that comes with trying to have the main meal and side dishes ready all at the same time.

Bread is the ideal partner for one-pot dishes. Not only do golden-crusted loaves fit the rustic, relaxed atmosphere that is part of the whole experience, but guests always enjoy tearing off chunks and using them to mop up every bit of the delicious sauce.

Above: Paella, a classic one-pot seafood and rice dish from Spain, is traditionally cooked in a shallow, two-handled pan.

Left: A whole chicken cooked with forty cloves of garlic makes the perfect pot-roast, and it, like other one-pot dishes, needs little attention once it is in the oven.

Below: Using a clay pot to cook one-pot recipes, such as this spinach and sweet potato dish, can be good for you. The clay pot ensures that the vitamins and minerals of the ingredients are retained.

There is also very little washing up, and if there are any leftovers, you may well be able to transform them into tasty pie fillings, simply by sandwiching them inside ready-rolled puff pastry or filo.

One-pot cooking is also extremely healthy, especially if you are using a clay pot. The pots ensure that most of the vitamins and minerals found in the ingredients are retained. This ancient form of cooking seals in the food's natural juices by enclosing it in a porous clay container that has been soaked in water. As the container heats up, the water turns to steam, keeping the contents moist and tender. The only other liquid used in clay-pot cooking is that which comes from the food itself, so that its full flavour can be appreciated.

Left: This spicy and aromatic Moroccan fish tagine is just one delicious fish dish that proves that fish is not only a wonderfully versatile and nutritious ingredient, but it should not be excluded from one-pot cooking.

Below: One-pot cooking doesn't have to take hours. Stir-fries are quick and easy to cook and are also wonderfully tasty.

If you have the time and the inclination you could make your own bread, matching the flavour of the central dish. For example, herb bread would be very welcome with Venison Sausages with Red Wine Gravy, while for something with a Mediterranean flavour, ciabatta or a bread made with sun-dried tomatoes would be ideal.

For one-pot dishes that already include starch, in the form of rice or potatoes, a simple salad might be a better choice as an accompaniment than bread. Try to include crisp ingredients, like fennel or celery, to provide a contrast in texture to the tenderness of the long-cooked meat or fish, and keep the dressing simple, so it does not vie with the flavours in the casserole or stew.

One-pot dishes also tend to be fairly good-natured, and will seldom spoil if not eaten the moment they are ready. Some dishes, like curries and casseroles, will improve if made the day before, so that all the flavours can bed down together and blend. Stir-fries, pasta and rice dishes need last-minute cooking, but if the preparation is done in advance, the effort is minimal.

One-pot cooking is perfect for everyone, from students with a single hot plate to families feeding in relays. Dishes can be cooked in the oven, on top of the stove or in a free-standing appliance like a microwave oven.

ONE-POT EQUIPMENT

If you are going to do a lot of cooking in just one pot, make it a good one. There's no point in planning a pot-roast for the whole family, only to find you haven't got a big enough pan, or that the one you have has a wobbly base. It is equally irritating to discover that your only decent casserole has a crack in it, or can only be used in the oven and not on top of the stove. Choose your cookware with care; it is worth investing in good quality equipment that will last.

Above: Frying pans with metal handles can be used under the grill (broiler) and in the oven.

Right: Stainless-steel pans with a heavy base are a good choice for one-pot cooking.

For one-pot cooking, you need a large pan with a heavy base, which will conduct the heat evenly and help to prevent the food from scorching should you inadvertently allow the amount of liquid to get too low. A good quality stainless-steel pan would be an excellent choice, but it is important to choose one with an aluminium or copper base, since stainless steel does not conduct heat well. For long, slow cooking, cast-iron pans coated in vitreous enamel are ideal, as they can also be used in the oven. When buying a frying pan, choose one with a heavy base. When cooking a frittata or a dessert such as tarte Tatin, it is essential to use a frying pan with a handle that can withstand the heat of the grill (broiler) or oven; a point worth considering when you are buying a new frying pan.

Woks

One of the most useful items in the kitchen, the wok need not be reserved solely for stir-frying. It is the ideal pan for quick-cooked creamy dishes such as beef Stroganoff. The wok can also be used for making a risotto. Woks that

Pots and Pans

When you are buying cooking equipment, it is very tempting to opt for a set of shiny pans, rather than individual items that might suit your purposes – and your personal circumstances – better.

Below left: A large pot with metal handles can be used on top of the stove and in the oven.

Left: Woks have either one or two handles.

Right: When buying casseroles, it is a good idea to choose different shapes and sizes.

Casseroles

For one-pot cooking, choose a casserole that is big enough to serve six, even if you usually cook for four. This will give you plenty of room for stirring the contents without risking splashes and scalds. The ideal pot will be one that can be used on top of the stove as well as inside it, so that if you do need to do any pre-cooking, or if cooking juices need to be reduced by boiling, you will not need a second container. If you buy several casseroles, vary the shapes as well as the sizes. For cooking a whole chicken, for instance, an oval is more useful than a round dish. Look at the handles, too. It is important that they are easy to grasp, and that they do not become so hot that they are liable to burn you, even when you are using an oven glove. Appearance will obviously be a consideration, since you will be serving straight from the casserole, but consider practical aspects too.

have a flat base can be used on all types of cooker. They can have either one or two handles. Those with two handles are good for deep-frying and general cooking, while the wok with one handle is designed especially for stir-frying. The single handle makes the wok easy to pick up so that the ingredients can be stirred and tossed in the wok at the same time.

Baking Dishes

There are plenty of one-pot recipes that benefit from being cooked in large, shallow dishes, from oven-roasted vegetables to layered potato bakes. Buy several different shapes, bearing in mind the size of your oven. Having two rectangular dishes that will fit side by side can be a real boon if you want to cook one meal for serving immediately and another for the freezer.

Ramekins

You will also find it useful to have six or eight ovenproof ramekin dishes, for baking single portions, such as individual soufflés and oven-baked desserts.

Below: Choose two ovenproof baking dishes that will fit next to each other in your oven.

FLAMEPROOF CASSEROLES

The most versatile casseroles are also flameproof and so can be used on top of the stove and under the grill (broiler) as well as in the oven.

ONE-POT COOKING TECHNIQUES

Cooking a dish in a single pot doesn't demand any particular expertise, but mastering a few simple techniques will make for greater efficiency, especially when preparing the ingredients. Many one-pot dishes need very little attention while they are actually cooking, but it is important to follow the instructions in individual recipes as regards stirring.

Stewing, Braising and Casseroling Meat
These are long, slow and moist methods of cooking either in the oven or on top of the stove. The meat is browned first to seal in the natural juices and improve the flavour and colour of the finished dish, then it is simmered slowly at a low temperature in liquid – wine, water, beer or stock.

1 Trim off any excess fat from the meat. For stewing and casseroling, cut the meat into 2.5cm/1in cubes. For braising use thickly cut steaks or cut the meat into thick slices.

2 Toss the meat a few pieces at a time in seasoned flour, then shake off any excess. The flour coating browns to give the casserole a good flavour and also thickens the liquid.

3 Heat 30ml/2 tbsp sunflower oil in a flameproof casserole. Add the meat in batches and cook over a high heat. When the meat is well browned on all sides, use a draining spoon to remove the meat before adding the next batch.

4 Add the sliced or chopped onions and other vegetables to the remaining fat and juices in the casserole and cook, stirring occasionally, for about 5 minutes.

5 Return the meat to the casserole, add herbs and pour in the cooking liquid. Stir to loosen the cooking residue from the base of the pan and then heat until simmering. Simmer gently on the hob or in the oven until the meat is tender. The casserole may be covered for the entire cooking time or uncovered towards the end to allow excess liquid to evaporate.

Pot-roasting Meat
This long, slow method of cooking is ideal for slightly tough joints of meat such as topside of beef, lamb shoulder and shanks, and knuckle of pork.

1 Heat a little sunflower oil in a large flameproof casserole until very hot. Add the meat and cook over a high heat, turning frequently, until browned on all sides. Remove the meat from the pan.

2 Add the onions, leeks and any root vegetables to the pan, then cook, stirring, for a few minutes. Replace the meat on top of the vegetables and pour in a little liquid, such as stock, wine or beer. Cover and cook gently in the oven until the meat is tender.

Casseroling Chicken

Moist cooking methods not only bring out the flavour of poultry but also offer the opportunity for allowing herbs and spices and aromatics to infuse the light meat thoroughly. Whole birds and joints can be casseroled.

I Brown the poutry pieces or bird all over first. Remove from the pan before softening chopped onion, carrot, celery and other flavouring ingredients in the fat remaining in the pan.

2 Replace the poultry before adding the chosen liquid – stock, wine or canned tomatoes. Season the casserole well, then bring it just to simmering point. Cover it closely and allow it to simmer very gently on top of the stove, or cook in the oven at 180°C/350°F/Gas 4.

COOKING TIMES FOR CASSEROLING CHICKEN

• For a whole bird allow 20 minutes per 450g/1lb, plus 20 minutes.
• Large portions 45–60 minutes.
• Boneless breasts about 30 minutes.
• Chunks or diced poultry 20–40 minutes, depending on their size.

Pan-frying Meat

This is the traditional cooking method for steaks such as sirloin and fillet, and it is also good for veal escalopes (US scallops) and veal chops, lamb chops, cutlets and noisettes, and pork chops, steaks and escalopes.

I Cook steaks and chops in the minimum of fat, then add flavoured butter when serving, if you like. Dab a little sunflower oil on kitchen paper and use to grease the pan lightly. Heat the pan until it is very hot (almost smoking). Add the steak or chops and cook for 2–4 minutes on each side.

2 Pan-fry other lean cuts of meat in a mixture of butter and oil. Butter burns easily, so heat the oil in the pan first and add the butter just before the meat to avoid this. Make sure that the butter and oil are sizzling before adding the meat. Cook on both sides until browned. Beef and thin cuts of meat such as escalopes will be ready to serve. For some thicker cuts and meat such as pork that needs to be well-cooked, reduce the heat to low once the meat is browned and cook for 10–15 minutes, or until cooked through. Test by piercing the centre of the meat with the point of a sharp knife.

Pan-frying Poultry

This quick cooking method is ideal for chicken breast fillets and portions. Once the meat is cooked, the cooking juices can be made into a tasty sauce, simply stir in a little cream, add some chopped herbs and season to taste.

When frying poultry, remember that it must be cooked through. Escalopes and boneless breasts cook quickly, so are ideal for pan-frying over a high heat, but uneven thicker portions require careful cooking. With larger pieces, reduce the heat to low once the chicken is browned and cook it slowly for up to 30 minutes to ensure that the centre is cooked.

Stir-frying

This is a fast method of cooking tender meat. The meat should be cut into thin slices across the grain, and then cut into fine, long strips. Use a wok or a heavy frying pan.

Heat a little oil in a wok or frying pan until it is smoking hot. Add the meat in batches and stir-fry over a high heat. Remove the cooked meat before adding a fresh batch. When all the meat is cooked, add the other ingredients and stir-fry over a slightly lower heat.

SOUPS

There's something supremely comforting about hot soup, and when you prepare it yourself, the aroma ensures that the pleasure starts long before you lift the ladle. Nourishing, easy to digest, quick to cook and convenient, soup provides the perfect meal-in-a-bowl at lunchtime or a warming after-school snack, and when served as a first course, it gives guests a real sense of welcome. Mediterranean Leek and Fish Soup with Tomatoes, Italian Farmhouse Soup, Seafood Chowder, and Lentil and Pasta Soup are just some of the treats in store.

LENTIL and PASTA SOUP

This rustic vegetarian soup makes a warming winter meal and goes especially well with Granary or crusty Italian bread.

SERVES 4–6

175g/6oz/¾ cup brown lentils
3 garlic cloves, unpeeled
1 litre/1¾ pints/4 cups water
45ml/3 tbsp olive oil
25g/1oz/2 tbsp butter
1 onion, finely chopped
2 celery sticks, finely chopped
30ml/2 tbsp sun-dried tomato
    purée (paste)
1.75 litres/3 pints/7½ cups vegetable stock
a few fresh marjoram leaves
a few fresh basil leaves
leaves from 1 fresh thyme sprig
50g/2oz/½ cup dried small pasta shapes,
    such as macaroni or tubetti
salt and ground black pepper
tiny fresh herb leaves, to garnish

1 Put the lentils in a large pan. Smash one of the garlic cloves using the blade of a large knife (there's no need to peel it first), then add it to the lentils. Pour in the water and bring to the boil. Simmer for about 20 minutes, or until the lentils are tender. Tip the lentils into a sieve, remove the garlic and set it aside. Rinse the lentils under the cold tap and leave to drain.

2 Heat 30ml/2 tbsp of the oil with half the butter in the pan. Add the onion and celery and cook gently for 5 minutes.

3 Crush the remaining garlic, then peel and mash the reserved garlic. Add to the pan with the remaining oil, the tomato purée and the lentils. Stir, then add the stock, herbs and salt and pepper. Bring to the boil, stirring. Simmer for 30 minutes, stirring occasionally.

4 Add the pasta and bring the soup back to the boil, stirring. Reduce the heat and simmer until the pasta is just tender. Add the remaining butter to the pan and stir until melted. Taste the soup for seasoning, then serve hot in warmed bowls, sprinkled with herb leaves.

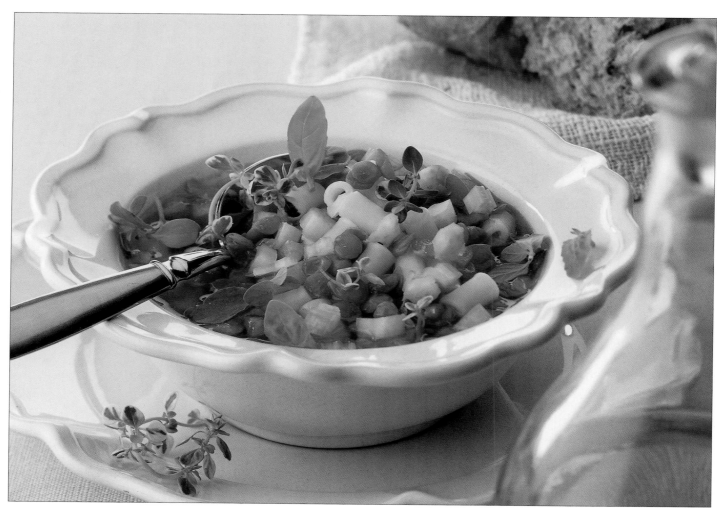

ITALIAN FARMHOUSE SOUP

Root vegetables form the base of this chunky, minestrone-style main meal soup. You can vary the vegetables according to what you have to hand.

SERVES 4

30ml/2 tbsp olive oil
1 onion, roughly chopped
3 carrots, cut into large chunks
175–200g/6–7oz turnips, cut into
    large chunks
about 175g/6oz swede (rutabaga), cut into
    large chunks
400g/14oz can chopped Italian tomatoes
15ml/1 tbsp tomato purée (paste)
5ml/1 tsp dried mixed herbs
5ml/1 tsp dried oregano
50g/2oz dried (bell) peppers, washed and
    thinly sliced (optional)
1.5 litres/2½ pints/6¼ cups vegetable stock
    or water
50g/2oz/½ cup dried small macaroni
    or conchiglie
400g/14oz can red kidney beans, rinsed
    and drained
30ml/2 tbsp chopped fresh flat leaf parsley
salt and ground black pepper
freshly grated Parmesan cheese, to serve

1 Heat the olive oil in a large pan, add the onion and cook over a low heat for about 5 minutes until softened. Add the carrot, turnip and swede chunks, canned chopped tomatoes, tomato purée, dried mixed herbs, dried oregano and dried peppers, if using. Stir in salt and pepper to taste.

2 Pour in the vegetable stock or water and bring to the boil. Stir well, cover the pan, then lower the heat and simmer for 30 minutes, stirring occasionally.

3 Add the pasta to the pan and bring quickly to the boil, stirring. Lower the heat and simmer, uncovered, for about 5 minutes until the pasta is only just tender, or according to the instructions on the packet. Stir frequently.

4 Stir in the kidney beans. Heat through for 2–3 minutes, then remove the pan from the heat and stir in the parsley. Taste the soup for seasoning. Serve hot in warmed soup bowls, with grated Parmesan cheese handed separately.

BROCCOLI, ANCHOVY and PASTA SOUP

This wonderfully chunky and flavourful soup is from Puglia in the south of Italy, where anchovies and broccoli are often used together.

SERVES 4

30ml/2 tbsp olive oil
1 garlic clove, finely chopped
¼–⅓ fresh red chilli, seeded and
    finely chopped
2 drained canned anchovies
1 small onion, finely chopped
200ml/7fl oz/scant 1 cup passata (bottled
    strained tomatoes)
45ml/3 tbsp dry white wine
1.2 litres/2 pints/5 cups vegetable or light
    chicken stock
300g/11oz broccoli florets
200g/7oz/1¾ cups dried orecchiette pasta
    or other medium-size pasta shapes
salt and ground black pepper
freshly grated Pecorino cheese, to serve

1 Heat the oil in a large pan. Add the garlic, chilli, anchovies and onion and cook over a low heat, stirring constantly, for 5–6 minutes.

2 Add the passata and wine, with salt and pepper to taste. Bring to the boil, cover, then cook over a low heat, stirring occasionally, for 12–15 minutes.

3 Pour in the stock. Bring to the boil, then add the broccoli and simmer for about 5 minutes. Add the pasta and bring back to the boil, stirring. Simmer, stirring frequently for 7–8 minutes until the pasta is just tender, or according to the packet instructions. Taste for seasoning. Serve hot, in warmed bowls. Hand around grated Pecorino separately.

PASTA SQUARES and PEAS in BROTH

This thick, filling Italian soup, flavoured with pancetta or bacon and prosciutto, is traditionally made with home-made pasta and fresh peas. In this modern, more convenient version, ready-made fresh lasagne sheets are used with frozen peas, to save time.

SERVES 4–6

25g/1oz/2 tbsp butter
50g/2oz pancetta or rindless smoked
    streaky (fatty) bacon, roughly chopped
1 small onion, finely chopped
1 celery stick, finely chopped
400g/14oz/3½ cups frozen peas
5ml/1 tsp tomato purée (paste)
5–10ml/1–2 tsp finely chopped fresh flat
    leaf parsley
1 litre/1¾ pints/4 cups chicken stock
300g/11oz fresh lasagne sheets
about 50g/2oz prosciutto, cut into cubes
salt and ground black pepper
freshly grated Parmesan cheese, to serve

1 Melt the butter in a large pan and add the pancetta or rindless smoked streaky bacon, with the chopped onion and chopped celery. Cook together over a low heat, stirring constantly, for 5 minutes.

2 Add the frozen peas to the pan and cook, stirring, for 3–4 minutes. Stir in the tomato purée and finely chopped parsley, then add the chicken stock, with salt and pepper to taste. Bring to the boil. Cover, lower the heat and simmer the soup for 10 minutes.

3 Meanwhile, using a large, sharp knife and a ruler, cut the lasagne sheets into 2cm/¾in squares.

4 Taste the soup for seasoning. Drop the pasta into the pan, then stir and bring to the boil. Simmer for 2 minutes, or until the pasta is just tender, then stir in the prosciutto. Serve hot with grated Parmesan handed around separately.

COOK'S TIP
Take care when seasoning the soup with salt, because of the saltiness of the pancetta and the prosciutto.

BOUILLABAISSE

Perhaps the most famous of all Mediterranean fish soups, this recipe, originating from Marseilles in the south of France, is a rich and colourful mixture of fish and shellfish, flavoured with tomatoes, saffron and orange.

SERVES 4–6

1.3–1.6kg/3–3½lb mixed fish and shellfish, such as red mullet, John Dory, monkfish, large prawns (shrimp) and clams
1.2 litres/2 pints/5 cups water
225g/8oz tomatoes
pinch of saffron threads
90ml/6 tbsp olive oil
1 onion, sliced
1 leek, sliced
1 celery stick, sliced
2 garlic cloves, crushed
bouquet garni
1 strip pared orange rind
2.5ml/½ tsp fennel seeds
15ml/1 tbsp tomato purée (paste)
10ml/2 tsp Pernod
4–6 thick slices French bread
45ml/3 tbsp chopped fresh parsley
salt and ground black pepper

1 Remove the heads, tails and fins from the fish and put in a large pan, with the water. Bring to the boil, and simmer for 15 minutes. Strain, and reserve the liquid.

2 Cut the fish into large chunks. Leave the shellfish in their shells.

3 Scald the tomatoes, then drain and refresh in cold water. Peel and chop them. Soak the saffron in 15–30ml/1–2 tbsp hot water. Heat the oil in the cleaned pan, add the onion, leek and celery and cook until softened. Add the garlic, bouquet garni, orange rind, fennel seeds and tomatoes, then stir in the saffron and liquid and the fish stock. Season with salt and pepper, then bring to the boil and simmer for 30–40 minutes.

4 Add the shellfish and boil for about 6 minutes. Discard any clams that remain closed. Add the fish and cook for a further 6–8 minutes until it flakes easily. Using a slotted spoon, transfer the fish to a warmed serving platter. Keep the liquid boiling and add the tomato purée and Pernod, then check the seasoning. Place a slice of bread in each soup bowl, pour the broth over and serve the fish separately, sprinkled with the parsley.

MEDITERRANEAN LEEK and FISH SOUP with TOMATOES

This chunky soup, which is almost a stew, makes a robust and wonderfully aromatic meal in a bowl. Serve it with crisp-toasted croûtes spread with a spicy garlic mayonnaise.

SERVES 4

30ml/2 tbsp olive oil
2 large thick leeks, white and green
    parts separated
5ml/1 tsp crushed coriander seeds
good pinch of dried red chilli flakes
300g/11oz small salad potatoes,
    thickly sliced
200g/7oz can chopped tomatoes
600ml/1 pint/2½ cups fish stock
150ml/¼ pint/⅔ cup fruity white wine
1 fresh bay leaf
1 star anise
1 strip pared orange rind
good pinch of saffron threads
450g/1lb white fish fillets, such as sea bass,
    monkfish, cod or haddock, skinned
450g/1lb small squid, cleaned
250g/9oz uncooked peeled
    prawns (shrimp)
30–45ml/2–3 tbsp chopped fresh parsley
salt and ground black pepper

For the garlic croûtes
1 short French loaf, sliced and toasted
spicy garlic mayonnaise

1 Gently heat the olive oil in a pan, then thinly slice the green part of the leeks. Add with the crushed coriander seeds and the dried red chilli flakes, and cook for 5 minutes, stirring occasionally.

2 Add the thickly sliced potatoes and chopped tomatoes and pour in the fish stock and white wine. Add the bay leaf, star anise, pared orange rind and saffron threads to the pan and stir well.

3 Bring to the boil, then reduce the heat and partly cover the pan. Simmer for about 20 minutes until the potatoes are tender. Taste and adjust the seasoning.

4 Cut the fish into chunks. Cut the squid sacs into rectangles and score a criss-cross pattern into them without cutting right through.

5 Add the fish to the soup, cook gently for 4 minutes, then add the prawns and cook for 1 minute. Add the squid and the thinly sliced white part of the leek and cook, stirring occasionally, for 2 minutes.

6 Stir in the chopped parsley and serve with the toasted croûtes topped with spicy garlic mayonnaise.

MEDITERRANEAN SAUSAGE and PESTO SOUP

This hearty soup makes a satisfying one-pot meal that brings the summery flavour of basil to midwinter meals. Thick slices of warm crusty bread make the perfect accompaniment.

SERVES 4

oil, for deep-frying
450g/1lb smoked pork sausages
a handful of fresh basil leaves
15ml/1 tbsp olive oil
1 red onion, chopped
225g/8oz/1 cup red lentils
400g/14oz can chopped tomatoes
 with herbs
1 litre/1¾ pints/4 cups chicken stock
 or water
salt and ground black pepper
60ml/4 tbsp pesto, to serve

COOK'S TIP
The flavour of smoked sausages is very good in this soup, but you could use ordinary fresh sausages if you like. Choose coarse-textured sausages, such as Toulouse.

1 Heat the oil for deep-frying to 190°C/375°F or until a cube of day-old bread browns in about 60 seconds. Slice one of the sausages diagonally and deep-fry for 2–3 minutes, or until brown and crisp. Add the basil leaves and fry for a few seconds until crisp. Lift out the sausage slices and basil leaves using a slotted spoon and drain them on kitchen paper. Strain the oil into a bowl.

2 Heat the olive oil in the pan, add the chopped red onion and cook until softened. Coarsely chop the remaining sausages and add them to the pan. Cook for about 5 minutes, stirring, or until the sausages are cooked.

3 Stir in the lentils, tomatoes and stock or water and bring to the boil. Reduce the heat, cover and simmer for about 20 minutes. Cool the soup slightly before puréeing it in a blender. Return the soup to the rinsed-out pan.

4 Reheat the soup, add seasoning to taste, then ladle into warmed individual soup bowls. Sprinkle the soup with the deep-fried sausage slices and basil and swirl a little pesto through each portion just before serving. Serve with plenty of warm crusty bread.

MOROCCAN SPICED LAMB SOUP

Classic north African spices — ginger, turmeric and cinnamon — are combined with chickpeas and lamb to make this hearty, warming soup.

SERVES 6

75g/3oz/½ cup chickpeas, soaked overnight
15g/½oz/1 tbsp butter
225g/8oz lamb, cut into cubes
1 onion, chopped
450g/1lb tomatoes, peeled and chopped
a few celery leaves, chopped
30ml/2 tbsp chopped fresh parsley
15ml/1 tbsp chopped fresh
    coriander (cilantro)
2.5ml/½ tsp ground ginger
2.5ml/½ tsp ground turmeric
5ml/1 tsp ground cinnamon
1.75 litres/3 pints/7½ cups water
75g/3oz/scant ½ cup green lentils
75g/3oz vermicelli or soup pasta
2 egg yolks
juice of ½–1 lemon
salt and ground black pepper
fresh coriander (cilantro), to garnish
lemon wedges, to serve

1 Drain the chickpeas, rinse under cold water and set aside. Melt the butter in a large flameproof casserole or pan and fry the lamb and onion for 2–3 minutes, stirring, until the lamb is just browned.

2 Add the chopped tomatoes, celery leaves, herbs and spices and season well with ground black pepper. Cook for about 1 minute, then stir in the water and add the green lentils and the soaked, drained and rinsed chickpeas.

3 Slowly bring to the boil and skim the surface to remove the froth. Boil rapidly for 10 minutes, then reduce the heat and simmer very gently for 2 hours, or until the chickpeas are very tender.

4 Season with salt and pepper, then add the vermicelli or soup pasta to the pan and cook for 5–6 minutes until it is just tender. If the soup is very thick at this stage, add a little more water.

5 Beat the egg yolks with the lemon juice and stir into the simmering soup. Immediately remove the soup from the heat and stir until thickened. Pour into warmed serving bowls and garnish with plenty of fresh coriander. Serve the soup with lemon wedges.

COOK'S TIP
If you have forgotten to soak the chickpeas overnight, place them in a pan with about four times their volume of cold water. Bring very slowly to the boil, then cover the pan, remove it from the heat and leave to stand for 45 minutes before using as described in the recipe.

CATALAN POTATO and BROAD BEAN SOUP

While they are in season fresh broad beans are perfect, but canned or frozen are just as good in this creamy, richly flavoured soup.

SERVES 6

30ml/2 tbsp olive oil
2 onions, chopped
3 large floury potatoes, diced
450g/1lb fresh shelled broad
    (fava) beans
1.75 litres/3 pints/7½ cups vegetable or
    chicken stock
1 bunch coriander (cilantro),
    finely chopped
150ml/¼ pint/⅔ cup single (light) cream
salt and ground black pepper
coriander (cilantro) leaves, to garnish

COOK'S TIP
Broad beans sometimes have a tough outer skin, particularly if they are large. To remove this, first cook the beans briefly in boiling water, then peel off the skin, and add the tender, bright green centre part to the soup.

1 Heat the olive oil in a large pan, add the chopped onions and fry, stirring occasionally with a wooden spoon, for about 5 minutes until they are just softened but not brown.

2 Add the diced potatoes, shelled broad beans (reserving a few for garnishing) and vegetable or chicken stock to the pan. Bring to the boil, then simmer for 5 minutes.

3 Stir in the finely chopped coriander and simmer for a further 10 minutes.

4 Process the soup in batches in a food processor or blender, then return the soup to the rinsed-out pan.

5 Stir in the cream (reserving a little for garnishing), season, and bring to a simmer. Serve garnished with more coriander leaves, beans and cream.

SPANISH POTATO and GARLIC SOUP

Traditionally served in shallow earthenware dishes, this delicious, classic Spanish soup is a great choice for vegetarians.

SERVES 6

30ml/2 tbsp olive oil
1 large onion, finely sliced
4 garlic cloves, crushed
1 large potato, halved and cut
    into thin slices
5ml/1 tsp paprika
400g/14oz can chopped tomatoes, drained
5ml/1 tsp thyme leaves, plus extra chopped
    thyme leaves, to garnish
900ml/1½ pints/3¾ cups vegetable stock
5ml/1 tsp cornflour (cornstarch)
salt and ground black pepper

COOK'S TIP
Paprika is a popular spice in many Spanish dishes. It is made from red peppers that are dried and powdered into a coarse-grained spice. It has a slightly sweet, mild flavour and a rich red colour.

1 Heat the oil in a large, heavy pan, add the onion, garlic, potato and paprika and cook, stirring occasionally, for about 5 minutes, or until the onions have softened, but not browned.

2 Add the chopped tomatoes, thyme leaves and vegetable stock to the pan and simmer for 15–20 minutes until the potatoes have cooked through.

3 In a small bowl, mix the cornflour with a little water to form a smooth paste, then stir into the soup. Bring to the boil, stirring, then simmer for about 5 minutes until the soup has thickened.

4 Using a wooden spoon, break up the potatoes slightly, then season to taste. Serve the soup garnished with the extra chopped thyme leaves.

CORN and POTATO CHOWDER

This creamy yet chunky soup is rich with the sweet taste of corn. It's excellent served with thick, crusty bread and topped with some grated Cheddar cheese.

2 Heat until the oil and butter are sizzling, then reduce the heat to low. Cover the pan and cook gently for about 10 minutes until the vegetables are just softened, shaking the pan occasionally.

3 Pour in the stock, season with salt and pepper to taste and bring to the boil. Reduce the heat, cover the pan again and simmer gently, stirring occasionally, for about 15 minutes, or until the vegetables are tender.

SERVES 4

1 onion, chopped
1 garlic clove, crushed
1 medium baking potato, chopped
2 celery sticks, sliced
1 green (bell) pepper, seeded and sliced
30ml/2 tbsp sunflower oil
25g/1oz/2 tbsp butter
600ml/1 pint/2½ cups vegetable stock
300ml/½ pint/1¼ cups milk
200g/7oz can flageolet, cannellini or
    haricot (navy) beans
300g/11oz can corn kernels
good pinch of dried sage
salt and ground black pepper
freshly grated Cheddar cheese, to serve

1 Put the onion, garlic, potato, celery and green pepper into a large, heavy pan with the sunflower oil and butter.

4 Add the milk, canned beans and corn kernels – including their liquids. Stir in the dried sage and simmer, uncovered, for 5 minutes, then check the seasoning and adjust to taste. Serve hot in bowls, sprinkled with the grated Cheddar cheese.

CLAM, MUSHROOM and POTATO CHOWDER

The delicate, sweet taste of clams and the soft earthiness of wild mushrooms combine
with potatoes to make this a great meal on its own — fit for any occasion.

SERVES 4

48 clams, scrubbed
50g/2oz/¼ cup unsalted (sweet)
    butter
1 large onion, chopped
1 celery stick, sliced
1 carrot, sliced
225g/8oz assorted wild and
    cultivated mushrooms
225g/8oz floury potatoes,
    thickly sliced
1.2 litres/2 pints/5 cups boiling light
    chicken or vegetable stock
1 thyme sprig
4 parsley stalks
salt and ground black pepper
thyme sprigs, to garnish

1 Place the clams in a large, heavy pan, discarding any that are open. Add 1cm/½in of water to the pan, then cover and bring to the boil. Cook over a medium heat for 6–8 minutes, shaking the pan occasionally, until the clams open (discard any clams that do not open).

2 Drain the clams over a bowl and remove most of the shells, leaving some in the shells as a garnish. Strain the cooking juices into the bowl, add all the clams and set aside.

3 Add the butter, onion, celery and carrot to the pan and cook gently until softened but not coloured. Add the mushrooms and cook for 3–4 minutes until their juices begin to appear. Add the potato slices, the clams and their juices, the stock, thyme and parsley stalks.

4 Bring to the boil, then reduce the heat, cover and simmer for 25 minutes. Season to taste, ladle into soup bowls, and garnish with thyme sprigs.

SEAFOOD CHOWDER

Chowder takes its name from the French word for cauldron – chaudière – the type of pot once traditionally used for soups and stews. Like most chowders, this is a substantial dish, which is good served with crusty bread for a lunch or supper.

SERVES 4–6

200g/7oz/generous 1 cup drained,
    canned corn kernels
600ml/1 pint/2½ cups milk
15g/½oz/1 tbsp butter
1 small leek, sliced
1 small garlic clove, crushed
2 rindless smoked streaky (fatty) bacon
    rashers (strips), finely chopped
1 small green or red (bell) pepper, seeded
    and diced
1 celery stick, chopped
115g/4oz/generous ½ cup white long
    grain rice
5ml/1 tsp plain (all-purpose) flour
about 450ml/¾ pint/scant 2 cups hot
    chicken or vegetable stock
4 large scallops
115g/4oz white fish fillet, such as monkfish,
    plaice or flounder
15ml/1 tbsp finely chopped fresh flat
    leaf parsley
good pinch of cayenne pepper
30–45ml/2–3 tbsp single (light)
    cream (optional)
salt and ground black pepper
crusty bread, to serve

1 Place half the drained corn kernels in a food processor or blender. Add a little of the milk and then process until the mixture is thick and creamy. Set aside.

COOK'S TIP
If you don't have a food processor, then simply chop the corn kernels finely and transfer to a bowl. Beat in the milk a little at time until the mixture is thick and creamy.

2 Melt the butter in a large, heavy pan. add the leek, garlic and bacon and gently fry for 4–5 minutes until the leek has softened but not browned.

3 Add the diced green or red pepper and the chopped celery and cook over a very gentle heat for 3–4 minutes more, stirring frequently, until the pepper and celery have softened slightly.

4 Stir in the rice and cook for a few minutes, stirring occasionally, until the grains begin to swell, then sprinkle the flour evenly over the top of the rice and vegetables. Cook for about 1 minute, stirring all the time, then gradually stir in the remaining milk and the hot stock.

VARIATIONS
You can use other shellfish in place of the scallops if you prefer – try fresh or frozen prawns (shrimp), or mussels or clams, which are equally good in or out of their shells. Allow frozen shellfish to thaw at room temperature before adding to the chowder. Undyed, naturally smoked haddock or cod would make a delicious alternative fish.

5 Bring the mixture to the boil over a medium heat, then lower the heat and stir in the creamed corn mixture, with the whole corn kernels. Season well.

6 Cover the pan and simmer very gently for about 20 minutes, or until the rice is tender, stirring occasionally. Add a little more chicken or vegetable stock or water to the pan if the mixture thickens too quickly or if the rice begins to stick to the base of the pan.

7 Cut the corals away from the scallops and set them aside, slice the white flesh into 5mm/¼in pieces. Cut the white fish fillet into bitesize chunks.

8 Add the scallops and chunks of fish to the chowder. Stir gently, then cook for 4 minutes.

9 Stir in the scallop corals, chopped parsley and cayenne pepper. Cook for a few minutes more until the scallops are just cooked and heated through, then stir in the cream, if using. Adjust the seasoning and serve the chowder with thick slices of crusty bread.

CHICKEN and LEEK SOUP with PRUNES and BARLEY

This recipe is based on the traditional Scottish soup, Cock-a-leekie. The unusual combination of leeks and prunes is surprisingly delicious.

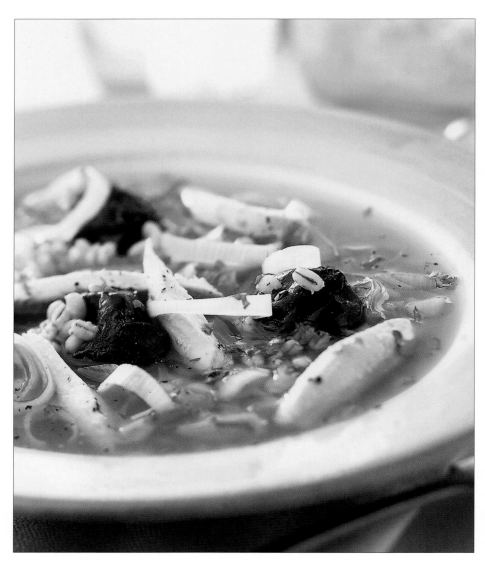

3 Bring the stock to the boil, then reduce the heat and cover the pan. Simmer gently for 1 hour. Skim off any scum when the water first starts to boil and occasionally during simmering.

4 Add the chicken breast portions to the pan and continue to cook for another 30 minutes until they are just cooked. Leave until cool enough to handle, then strain the stock. Reserve the chicken breast portions and the meat from the carcass. Discard all the skin, bones, cooked vegetables and herbs. Skim as much fat as you can from the stock, then return it to the pan.

5 Add the pearl barley to the stock. Bring to the boil over a medium heat, then lower the heat and cook very gently for 15–20 minutes, until the barley is just cooked and tender. Season the soup with 5ml/1 tsp each salt and ground black pepper.

SERVES 6

115g/4oz/⅔ cup pearl barley
1 chicken, weighing about 2kg/4¼lb
900g/2lb leeks
1 fresh bay leaf
a few fresh parsley stalks and
    thyme sprigs
1 large carrot, thickly sliced
2.4 litres/4 pints/10 cups chicken or
    beef stock
400g/14oz ready-to-eat prunes
salt and ground black pepper
chopped fresh parsley, to garnish

1 Rinse the pearl barley thoroughly in a sieve under cold running water, then cook it in a large pan of boiling water for about 10 minutes. Drain the barley, rinse well again and drain thoroughly. Set aside in a cool place.

2 Cut the breast portions off the chicken and set aside, then place the remaining chicken carcass in the pan. Cut half the leeks into 5cm/2in lengths and add them to the pan. Tie the herbs together into a bouquet garni and add to the pan with the carrot and stock.

6 Add the ready-to-eat prunes to the pan, then thinly slice the remaining leeks and add them to the pan. Bring to the boil, then cover the pan and simmer gently for about 10 minutes, or until the leeks are just cooked.

7 Slice the chicken breast portions and then add them to the soup with the remaining chicken meat from the carcass, sliced or cut into neat pieces. Reheat the soup, if necessary, then ladle it into warm, deep soup plates and sprinkle with plenty of chopped parsley to serve.

COCONUT and SEAFOOD SOUP with GARLIC CHIVES

The long list of ingredients in this Thai-inspired recipe could mislead you into thinking that this soup is complicated. In fact, it is very easy to put together.

SERVES 4

600ml/1 pint/2½ cups fish stock
5 thin slices fresh root ginger
2 lemon grass stalks, chopped
3 kaffir lime leaves, shredded
25g/1oz garlic chives (1 bunch), chopped
15g/½oz fresh coriander (cilantro)
15ml/1 tbsp vegetable oil
4 shallots, chopped
400ml/14fl oz can coconut milk
30–45ml/2–3 tbsp Thai fish sauce
45–60ml/3–4 tbsp Thai green curry paste
450g/1lb uncooked large prawns (jumbo shrimp), peeled and deveined
450g/1lb prepared squid
a little lime juice (optional)
salt and ground black pepper
60ml/4 tbsp fried shallot slices, to serve

1 Pour the stock into a pan and add the slices of fresh ginger, the chopped lemon grass and half the lime leaves.

2 Add half the chopped chives to the pan with the coriander stalks. Bring to the boil, then reduce the heat. Cover the pan, then simmer gently for 20 minutes. Strain the stock.

3 Rinse the pan, then add the oil and shallots. Cook over a medium heat for 5–10 minutes, stirring occasionally, until the shallots are just beginning to brown. Stir in the stock, coconut milk, the remaining lime leaves and half the fish sauce. Heat gently until the soup is just simmering and cook over a low heat for 5–10 minutes.

4 Stir in the curry paste and the peeled prawns and cook for 3 minutes. Add the squid, cook for a further 2 minutes. Add the lime juice, if using, and season.

5 Stir in the remaining fish sauce, chopped chives and the chopped coriander leaves. Serve in warmed, shallow bowls sprinkled with fried shallots.

VARIATIONS
• Instead of squid, you could add 400g/14oz firm white fish, such as monkfish, cut into small pieces.
• You could also replace the squid with fresh mussels. Steam 675g/1½lb closed mussels in a tightly covered pan for about 3 minutes, or until the shells have opened. Discard any that remain shut, then remove the mussels from their shells.

MEAT AND GAME MAIN MEALS

This chapter lifts the lid on delicious main courses made effortlessly in one pot. You'll be reminded of old favourites like Toad-in-the-Hole and Pork Chow Mein, and invited to try some exciting new flavours, such as Ostrich Stew with Sweet Potatoes and Chickpeas, or Grouse with Orchard Fruit Stuffing. For a wonderful experience you'll be sure to repeat, try Pancetta and Broad Bean Risotto or Spiced Lamb with Tomatoes and Peppers.

SWEET-and-SOUR PORK STIR-FRY

This is a great idea for a quick family supper. Remember to cut the carrots into thin matchstick strips so that they cook in time.

SERVES 4

450g/1lb pork fillet (tenderloin)
30ml/2 tbsp plain (all-purpose) flour
45ml/3 tbsp oil
1 onion, roughly chopped
1 garlic clove, crushed
1 green (bell) pepper, seeded and sliced
350g/12oz carrots, cut into thin strips
225g/8oz can bamboo shoots, drained
15ml/1 tbsp white wine vinegar
15ml/1 tbsp soft brown sugar
10ml/2 tsp tomato purée (paste)
30ml/2 tbsp light soy sauce
salt and ground black pepper

1 Thinly slice the pork. Season the flour and toss the pork in it to coat.

2 Heat the oil in a wok or large frying pan and cook the pork over a medium heat for about 5 minutes, until golden and cooked through. Remove the pork with a slotted spoon and drain on kitchen paper. You may need to do this in several batches.

3 Add the onion and garlic to the pan and cook for 3 minutes. Stir in the pepper and carrots and stir-fry over a high heat for 6–8 minutes, or until beginning to soften slightly.

4 Return the meat to the pan with the bamboo shoots. Add the remaining ingredients with 120ml/4fl oz/½ cup water and bring to the boil. Simmer gently for 2–3 minutes, or until piping hot. Adjust the seasoning, if necessary, and serve immediately.

VARIATION
Finely sliced strips of skinless chicken breast fillet can be used in this recipe instead of the pork.

PORK CHOW MEIN

This is a very speedy dish to cook, but make sure that you prepare all the ingredients
before you start to cook. If you don't have a wok, use a very large frying pan instead.

SERVES 4

175g/6oz medium egg noodles
350g/12oz pork fillet (tenderloin)
30ml/2 tbsp sunflower oil
15ml/1 tbsp sesame oil
2 garlic cloves, crushed
8 spring onions (scallions), sliced
1 red (bell) pepper, seeded and
    roughly chopped
1 green (bell) pepper, seeded and
    roughly chopped
30ml/2 tbsp dark soy sauce
45ml/3 tbsp dry sherry
175g/6oz/¾ cup beansprouts
45ml/3 tbsp chopped fresh flat leaf parsley
15ml/1 tbsp toasted sesame seeds

1 Soak the noodles according to the
packet instructions, then drain well.

2 Thinly slice the pork fillet. Heat the
sunflower oil in a wok or large frying pan
and cook the pork over a high heat until
golden brown and cooked through.

3 Add the sesame oil to the pan, with
the garlic, spring onions and peppers.
Cook over a high heat for 3–4 minutes,
or until beginning to soften.

4 Reduce the heat slightly, then stir in
the soaked noodles, with the dark soy
sauce and dry sherry. Stir-fry for about
2 minutes. Add the beansprouts and
cook for a further 1–2 minutes. If the
noodles begin to stick to the pan, add
a splash of water. Stir in the chopped
parsley and serve the chow mein
sprinkled with the toasted sesame seeds.

PORK COOKED in CIDER with PARSLEY DUMPLINGS

Pork and fruit are a perfect combination. If you don't want to make dumplings, serve creamy mashed potatoes with the stew.

SERVES 6

115g/4oz/½ cup pitted prunes,
    roughly chopped
115g/4oz/½ cup ready-to-eat dried
    apricots, roughly chopped
300ml/½ pint/1¼ cups dry (hard) cider
30ml/2 tbsp plain (all-purpose) flour
675g/1½lb lean boneless pork, cut
    into cubes
30ml/2 tbsp vegetable oil
350g/12oz onions, roughly chopped
2 garlic cloves, crushed
6 celery sticks, roughly chopped
475ml/16fl oz/2 cups stock
12 juniper berries, lightly crushed
30ml/2 tbsp chopped fresh thyme
425g/15oz can black-eyed beans
    (peas), drained
salt and ground black pepper

For the dumplings
115g/4oz/1 cup self-raising (self-rising) flour
50g/2oz/scant ½ cup vegetable suet
45ml/3 tbsp chopped fresh parsley
90ml/6 tbsp water

1 Preheat the oven to 180°C/350°F/ Gas 4. Place the roughly chopped prunes and apricots in a small bowl. Pour over the cider and leave to soak for at least 20 minutes.

VARIATION
This recipe can also be made with lean lamb – leg steaks or diced shoulder would be ideal cuts to choose. Omit the juniper berries, try cannellini beans in place of the black-eyed beans and use red onions rather than brown ones.

2 Season the flour, then toss the pork in the flour to coat. Reserve any leftover flour. Heat the oil in a large flameproof casserole. Brown the meat in batches, adding a little more oil if necessary. Remove the meat with a slotted spoon and drain on kitchen paper.

3 Add the onions, garlic and celery to the casserole and cook for 5 minutes. Add any reserved flour and cook for a further 1 minute.

4 Blend in the stock until smooth. Add the cider and fruit, juniper berries, thyme and plenty of seasoning. Bring to the boil, add the pork, cover tightly and then cook in the oven for 50 minutes.

5 Just before the end of the cooking time prepare the dumplings. Sift the flour into a large bowl, add a pinch of salt, then stir in the suet and chopped fresh parsley. Add the water gradually and mix all the ingredients together to form a smooth, slightly sticky dough.

6 Remove the casserole from the oven, then stir in the black-eyed beans and adjust the seasoning. Divide the dumpling mixture into six, form into rough rounds and place on top of the stew. Return the casserole to the oven, then cover and cook for a further 20–25 minutes, or until the dumplings are cooked and the pork is tender.

COOK'S TIP
Black-eyed beans or peas, as they are called in America, are also sometimes referred to as cowpeas. They are a medium-size cream-coloured bean with a distinctive black spot or "eye" on the inner curve. They have a smooth, creamy texture and a subtle flavour. Black-eyed beans are a popular addition to soups and casseroles and are widely used in southern American cuisines.

POT-ROAST LOIN of PORK with APPLE

Roasted pork loin with crisp crackling and a lightly spiced apple and raisin stuffing makes a wonderful Sunday-lunch main course.

SERVES 6–8

1.8kg/4lb boned loin of pork
300ml/½ pint/1¼ cups dry (hard) cider
150ml/¼ pint/⅔ cup sour cream
7.5ml/1½ tsp salt

For the stuffing
25g/1oz/2 tbsp butter
1 small onion, chopped
50g/2oz/1 cup fresh white breadcrumbs
2 apples, cored, peeled and chopped
50g/2oz/scant ½ cup raisins
finely grated rind of 1 orange
pinch of ground cloves
salt and ground black pepper

1 Preheat the oven to 220°C/425°F/ Gas 7. To make the stuffing, melt the butter in a frying pan and gently fry the onion for 10 minutes until soft. Stir in the remaining stuffing ingredients.

2 Put the pork, rind side down, on a board. Make a horizontal cut between the meat and outer layer of fat, cutting to within 2.5cm/1in of the edges to make a pocket.

3 Push the prepared stuffing into the pocket. Roll up the pork lengthwise and tie firmly with string. Score the rind at 2cm/¾in intervals with a sharp knife.

4 Pour the cider and sour cream into a large casserole. Stir to combine, then add the pork, rind-side down. Transfer to the oven and cook, uncovered, for 30 minutes.

5 Turn the joint over, so that the rind is on top. Baste with the juices, then sprinkle the rind with salt. Cook for a further 1 hour, basting after 30 minutes. Reduce the oven temperature to 180°C/ 350°F/Gas 4. Cook for 1½ hours, then remove the casserole from the oven and leave the joint to stand for 20 minutes before carving.

COOK'S TIP
Do not baste during the final 1½ hours of roasting, so the crackling becomes crisp.

NOISETTES of PORK with CREAMY CALVADOS and APPLE SAUCE

This dish gives the impression of being far more difficult to prepare than it really is, so it is ideal as part of a formal menu to impress guests. Buttered gnocchi or griddled polenta and red cabbage are suitable accompaniments.

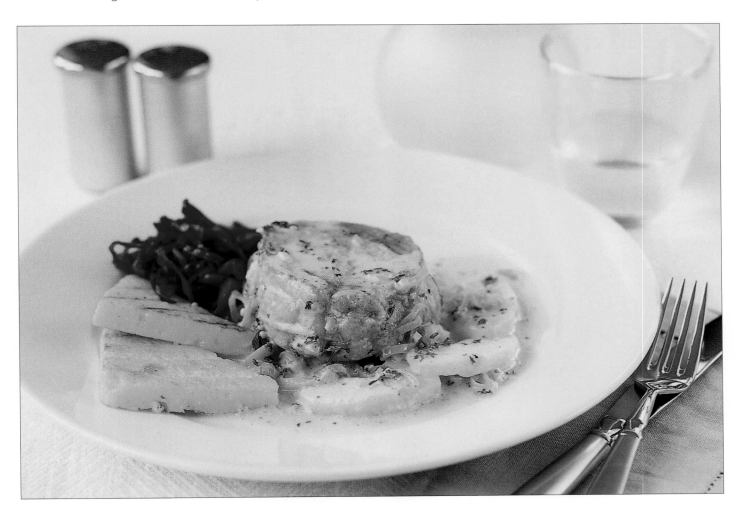

SERVES 4

30ml/2 tbsp plain (all-purpose) flour
4 noisettes of pork, about 175g/6oz each, firmly tied
25g/1oz/2 tbsp butter
4 baby leeks, finely sliced
5ml/1 tsp mustard seeds, coarsely crushed
30ml/2 tbsp Calvados
150ml/¼ pint/⅔ cup dry white wine
2 eating apples, peeled, cored and sliced
150ml/¼ pint/⅔ cup double (heavy) cream
30ml/2 tbsp chopped fresh flat leaf parsley
salt and ground black pepper

1 Place the flour in a bowl and add plenty of seasoning. Turn the noisettes in the flour mixture to coat them lightly.

2 Melt the butter in a heavy frying pan and cook the noisettes until golden on both sides. Remove from the pan and set aside.

3 Add the leeks to the fat remaining in the pan and cook for 5 minutes. Stir in the mustard seeds and pour in the Calvados, then carefully ignite it to burn off the alcohol. When the flames have died down, pour in the wine and replace the pork. Cook gently for 10 minutes, turning the pork frequently.

4 Add the sliced apples to the pan and pour in the cream. Simmer for about 5 minutes, or until the apples are tender and the sauce is thick and creamy. Taste for seasoning, then stir in the chopped fresh parsley and serve immediately.

BRAZILIAN PORK and RICE CASSEROLE

We tend to associate Brazil with beef recipes, but there are also some excellent pork recipes, including this hearty dish of marinated pork, vegetables and rice.

SERVES 4–6

500g/1¼lb lean pork, such as fillet (tenderloin), cut into strips
60ml/4 tbsp vegetable oil
1 onion, chopped
1 garlic clove, crushed
1 green (bell) pepper, cut into pieces
about 300ml/½ pint/1¼ cups chicken or vegetable stock
225g/8oz/generous 1 cup white long grain rice
150ml/¼ pint/⅔ cup single (light) cream
150g/5oz/1½ cups freshly grated Parmesan cheese
salt and ground black pepper

For the marinade
120ml/4fl oz/½ cup dry white wine
30ml/2 tbsp lemon juice
1 onion, chopped
4 juniper berries, lightly crushed
3 cloves
1 fresh red chilli, seeded and finely sliced

1 Mix the marinade ingredients in a shallow dish, add the pork strips and leave to marinate for 3–4 hours, stirring occasionally. Transfer the pork to a plate using a slotted spoon and pat dry. Strain the marinade and set aside.

2 Heat the oil in a heavy pan, add the pork strips and fry for a few minutes until evenly brown. Transfer to a plate using a slotted spoon.

3 Add the chopped onion and the garlic to the pan and fry for 3–4 minutes. Stir in the pieces of pepper and cook for 3–4 minutes more, then return the pork strips to the pan. Pour in the reserved marinade and the stock. Bring to the boil and season with salt and pepper, then lower the heat, cover the pan and simmer gently for 10 minutes, or until the meat is nearly tender.

VARIATION
Strips of chicken breast meat can be used in this recipe instead of the lean pork fillet.

4 Preheat the oven to 160°C/325°F/ Gas 3. Cook the rice in plenty of lightly salted boiling water for 8 minutes or until three-quarters cooked. Drain well. Spread half the rice over the base of a buttered, earthenware dish. Using a slotted spoon, make a neat layer of meat and vegetables on top, then spread over the remaining rice.

5 Stir the cream and 30ml/2 tbsp of the grated Parmesan into the liquid in which the pork was cooked. Tip into a jug (pitcher) and then carefully pour the cream mixture over the rice and sprinkle with the remaining Parmesan. Cover with foil and bake for 20 minutes, then remove the foil and cook for 5 minutes more, until the top is lightly brown.

TOAD-in-the-HOLE

This is one of those dishes that is classic comfort food — perfect for lifting the spirits on cold days. Use only the best sausages for this grown-up version, which includes chives.

SERVES 4–6

175g/6oz/1½ cups plain (all-purpose) flour
30ml/2 tbsp chopped fresh chives (optional)
2 eggs
300ml/½ pint/1¼ cups milk
50g/2oz/⅓ cup white vegetable fat
    or lard
450g/1lb Cumberland sausages or good-
    quality pork sausages
salt and ground black pepper

VARIATION

For a young children's supper, make small individual toad-in-the-holes: omit the chopped fresh chives from the batter and cook small cocktail sausages in patty tins (muffin pans) until golden. **Add the batter and cook for 10–15 minutes, or until puffed and golden brown.**

1 Preheat the oven to 220°C/425°F/ Gas 7. Sift the flour into a bowl with a pinch of salt and pepper. Make a well in the centre of the flour. Whisk the chives, if using, with the eggs and milk, then pour this into the well in the flour. Gradually whisk the flour into the liquid to make a smooth batter. Cover and leave to stand for at least 30 minutes.

2 Put the vegetable fat or lard into a small roasting pan and place in the oven for 3–5 minutes until very hot. Add the sausages and cook for 15 minutes. Turn the sausages twice during cooking.

3 Pour the batter over the sausages and cook for about 20 minutes, or until the batter is risen and golden. Serve immediately.

PANCETTA and BROAD BEAN RISOTTO

This delicious risotto makes a healthy and filling meal, when served with a mixed green salad. Use smoked bacon instead of pancetta, if you like.

SERVES 4

225g/8oz frozen baby broad (fava) beans
15ml/1 tbsp olive oil
1 onion, chopped
2 garlic cloves, finely chopped
175g/6oz smoked pancetta, diced
350g/12oz/1¾ cups risotto rice
1.2 litres/2 pints/5 cups chicken stock
30ml/2 tbsp chopped fresh mixed herbs,
    such as parsley, thyme and oregano
salt and ground black pepper
coarsely chopped fresh parsley, to garnish
shavings of Parmesan cheese, to serve
    (see Cook's Tip)

1 First, cook the broad beans in a large flameproof casserole of lightly salted boiling water for about 3 minutes until tender. Drain and set aside.

2 Heat the olive oil in the casserole. Add the chopped onion, chopped garlic and diced pancetta and cook gently for about 5 minutes, stirring occasionally.

3 Add the rice to the pan and cook for 1 minute, stirring. Add 300ml/½ pint/ 1¼ cups of the stock and simmer, stirring frequently until it has been absorbed.

4 Continue adding the stock, a ladleful at a time, stirring frequently until the rice is just tender and creamy, and almost all of the liquid has been absorbed. This will take 30–35 minutes. It may not be necessary to add all the stock.

5 Stir the beans, mixed herbs and seasoning into the risotto. Heat gently, then serve garnished with the chopped fresh parsley and sprinkled with shavings of Parmesan cheese.

COOK'S TIP

To make thin Parmesan cheese shavings, take a rectangular block or long wedge of Parmesan and firmly scrape a vegetable peeler down the side of the cheese to make shavings. The swivel-bladed type of peeler is best for this job.

PAN-FRIED HAM and VEGETABLES
with EGGS

A perfect family supper dish, this is very easy to prepare. Serve with plenty of hot,
crusty bread: Italian ciabatta is particularly good.

3 Add the courgettes and peppers to the onion and garlic and cook over a medium heat for 3–4 minutes.

4 Stir in the paprika, tomatoes, tomato purée, ham and seasoning. Bring to the boil and simmer gently for 15 minutes.

5 Reduce the heat to low. Make four wells in the tomato mixture, break an egg into each and season. Cook over a gentle heat until the white begins to set.

6 Preheat the grill (broiler). Sprinkle the cheese over the vegetables and grill (broil) for about 5 minutes until the eggs are set. Serve immediately with bread.

SERVES 4

30ml/2 tbsp olive oil
1 onion, roughly chopped
2 garlic cloves, crushed
175g/6oz cooked ham
225g/8oz courgettes (zucchini)
1 red (bell) pepper, seeded and
   thinly sliced
1 yellow (bell) pepper, seeded and
   thinly sliced
10ml/2 tsp paprika
400g/14oz can chopped tomatoes
15ml/1 tbsp sun-dried tomato purée (paste)
4 eggs
115g/4oz/1 cup coarsely grated
   Cheddar cheese
salt and ground black pepper
crusty bread, to serve

1 Heat the olive oil in a deep frying pan. Add the onion and garlic and cook for 4 minutes, stirring frequently, or until just beginning to soften.

2 While the onions and garlic are cooking, cut the ham and courgettes into 5cm/2in long batons. Set the ham aside.

MINTED LAMB STIR-FRY

Lamb and mint have a long-established partnership that works particularly well in this full-flavoured stir-fry. Serve with plenty of crusty bread.

SERVES 2

275g/10oz lamb neck fillet or boneless
　　leg steaks
30ml/2 tbsp sunflower oil
10ml/2 tsp sesame oil
1 onion, roughly chopped
2 garlic cloves, crushed
1 red chilli, seeded and
　　finely chopped
75g/3oz fine green beans, halved
225g/8oz fresh spinach, shredded
30ml/2 tbsp oyster sauce
30ml/2 tbsp Thai fish sauce (*nam pla*)
15ml/1 tbsp lemon juice
5ml/1 tsp sugar
45ml/3 tbsp chopped fresh mint
salt and ground black pepper
mint sprigs, to garnish
noodles or rice, to serve

1 Trim the lamb of any excess fat and cut into thin slices. Heat the sunflower and sesame oils in a wok or large frying pan and cook the lamb over a high heat until browned. Remove with a slotted spoon and drain on kitchen paper.

2 Add the onion, garlic and chilli to the wok, cook for 2–3 minutes, then add the beans and stir-fry for 3 minutes.

3 Stir in the shredded spinach with the browned meat, oyster sauce, Thai fish sauce, lemon juice and sugar. Stir-fry for a further 3–4 minutes, or until the lamb is cooked through.

4 Sprinkle in the chopped mint and toss lightly, then adjust the seasoning. Serve piping hot, garnished with mint sprigs and accompanied by noodles or rice.

SPICED LAMB with TOMATOES and PEPPERS

Select lean tender lamb from the leg for this lightly spiced curry with juicy peppers and wedges of onion. Serve warm naan bread to mop up the tomato-rich juices.

3 Cut two of the onions into wedges (six from each onion) and add to the oil remaining in the pan. Fry the onions over a medium heat for 10 minutes, or until they are beginning to colour. Add the peppers and cook for 5 minutes. Use a slotted spoon to remove the vegetables from the pan and set aside.

4 Meanwhile, chop the remaining onion. Add it to the oil remaining in the pan with the chopped garlic, chilli and ginger, and cook for 4–5 minutes, stirring frequently, until the onion has softened.

5 Stir in the curry paste and canned tomatoes with the reserved yogurt. Return the lamb to the pan, season and stir well. Bring to the boil, then reduce the heat and simmer for 30 minutes.

SERVES 6

1.5kg/3¼lb lean boneless lamb, cubed
250ml/8fl oz/1 cup natural (plain) yogurt
30ml/2 tbsp sunflower oil
3 onions
2 red (bell) peppers, seeded and cut
   into chunks
3 garlic cloves, finely chopped
1 red chilli, seeded and chopped
2.5cm/1in piece fresh root ginger, peeled
   and chopped
30ml/2 tbsp mild curry paste
2 × 400g/14oz cans chopped tomatoes
large pinch of saffron threads
800g/1¾lb plum tomatoes, halved, seeded
   and cut into chunks
salt and ground black pepper
chopped fresh coriander (cilantro),
   to garnish

1 Mix the lamb with the yogurt in a bowl. Cover and chill for about 1 hour.

2 Heat the oil in a large pan. Drain the lamb and reserve the yogurt, then cook the lamb in batches until it is golden on all sides – this will take about 15 minutes in total. Remove the lamb from the pan using a slotted spoon and set aside.

6 Pound the saffron to a powder in a mortar, then stir in a little boiling water to dissolve the saffron. Add this liquid to the curry and stir well. Return the onion and pepper mixture to the pan, then stir in the fresh tomatoes. Bring the curry back to simmering point and cook for 15 minutes. Garnish with chopped fresh coriander to serve.

IRISH STEW

Simple and delicious, this is the quintessential Irish main course. Traditionally, mutton chops are used, but as they are harder to find these days you can use lamb instead.

SERVES 4

1.3kg/3lb boneless lamb chops, cut into
    large chunks
15ml/1 tbsp vegetable oil
3 onions
4 large carrots
900ml/1½ pints/3¾ cups water
4 large potatoes, cut into
    large chunks
1 large fresh thyme sprig
15g/½oz/1 tbsp unsalted
    (sweet) butter
15ml/1 tbsp chopped fresh parsley
salt and ground black pepper

1 Trim any fat from the lamb. Heat the oil in a large, flameproof casserole and brown the meat on all sides. Remove from the casserole.

2 Cut the onions into quarters and thickly slice the carrots. Add them to the casserole and cook for 5 minutes, stirring, or until the onions are browned. Return the meat to the pan with the water. Bring to the boil, reduce the heat, cover and simmer for 1 hour.

3 Add the potatoes to the pan with the thyme and cook for a further 1 hour.

4 Leave the stew to settle for a few minutes. Remove the fat from the liquid with a spoon, then stir in the butter and the parsley. Season well before serving.

LAMB and PUMPKIN COUSCOUS

Pumpkin is a very popular Moroccan ingredient and this is a traditional couscous recipe, with echoes of the very early vegetable couscous dishes made by the Berbers.

2 Cut the lamb into bitesize pieces and place in the pan with the sliced onions, and add the saffron, ginger, turmeric, pepper and salt. Pour in the water and stir well, then slowly bring to the boil. Cover the pan and simmer for about 1 hour until the meat is tender.

3 Peel or scrape the carrots and cut them into large chunks. Cut the pumpkin into 2.5cm/1in cubes, discarding the skin, seeds and pith.

4 Stir the carrots, pumpkin and raisins into the meat mixture with the chickpeas, cover the pan and simmer for 30–35 minutes more, stirring occasionally, until the vegetables and meat are completely tender.

5 Meanwhile, prepare the couscous according to the instructions on the packet and steam on top of the stew, then fork lightly to fluff up. Spoon the couscous on to a warmed serving plate, add the stew and stir the stew into the couscous. Extra gravy can be served separately. Sprinkle some tiny sprigs of fresh parsley over the top and serve immediately.

SERVES 4–6

75g/3oz/½ cup chickpeas, soaked overnight and drained
675g/1½lb lean lamb
2 large onions, sliced
pinch of saffron threads
1.5ml/¼ tsp ground ginger
2.5ml/½ tsp ground turmeric
5ml/1 tsp ground black pepper
1.2 litres/2 pints/5 cups water
450g/1lb carrots
675g/1½lb pumpkin
75g/3oz/⅔ cup raisins
400g/14oz/2¼ cups couscous
salt
sprigs of fresh parsley, to garnish

1 Place the chickpeas in a large pan of boiling water. Boil for 10 minutes, then reduce the heat and cook for 1–1½ hours until tender. Place in cold water and remove the skins by rubbing with your fingers. Discard the skins and drain.

BRAISED SHOULDER of LAMB with PEARL BARLEY and BABY VEGETABLES

In this wonderful, slow-cooked stew, the pearl barley absorbs all the rich meat juices and stock to become full-flavoured and nutty in texture when cooked.

SERVES 4

60ml/4 tbsp olive oil
1 large onion, chopped
2 garlic cloves, chopped
2 celery sticks, sliced
a little plain (all-purpose) flour
675g/1½lb boned shoulder of lamb, cut into cubes
900ml–1 litre/1½–1¾ pints/3¾–4 cups lamb stock
115g/4oz/⅔ cup pearl barley
225g/8oz baby carrots
225g/8oz baby turnips
salt and ground black pepper
30ml/2 tbsp chopped fresh marjoram, to garnish

1 Heat 45ml/3 tbsp of the oil in a flameproof casserole. Cook the onion and garlic until softened, add the celery, then cook until the vegetables brown.

2 Season the flour and toss the lamb in it. Use a slotted spoon to remove the vegetables from the casserole.

3 Add and heat the remaining oil with the juices in the casserole. Brown the lamb in batches until golden. When all the meat is browned, return it to the casserole with the onion mixture. Stir in 900ml/1½ pints/3¾ cups of the stock. Add the pearl barley. Cover, then bring to the boil, reduce the heat and simmer for 1 hour, or until the pearl barley and lamb are tender.

4 Add the baby carrots and turnips to the casserole for the final 15 minutes of cooking. Stir the meat occasionally during cooking and add the remaining stock, if necessary. Stir in seasoning to taste, and serve piping hot, garnished with marjoram. Warm, crusty bread would make a good accompaniment.

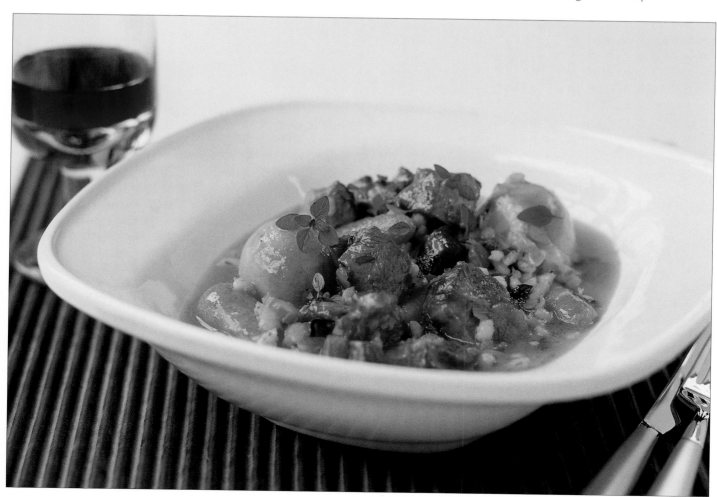

BRAISED LAMB with APRICOTS and HERB DUMPLINGS

A rich and fruity lamb casserole, topped with light, herby dumplings, which is delicious served with baked potatoes and broccoli.

SERVES 6

30ml/2 tbsp sunflower oil
675g/1½lb lean lamb fillet, cut into
    2.5cm/1in cubes
350g/12oz baby (pearl) onions, peeled
1 garlic clove, crushed
225g/8oz/3 cups button
    (white) mushrooms
175g/6oz/¾ cup small ready-to-eat
    dried apricots
about 250ml/8fl oz/1 cup well-flavoured
    lamb or beef stock
250ml/8fl oz/1 cup red wine
15ml/1 tbsp tomato purée (paste)
salt and ground black pepper
fresh herb sprigs, to garnish

For the dumplings
115g/4oz/1 cup self-raising
    (self-rising) flour
50g/2oz/scant ½ cup shredded
    vegetable suet
15–30ml/1–2 tbsp chopped fresh
    mixed herbs

1 Preheat the oven to 160°C/325°F/ Gas 3. Heat the oil in a large, flameproof casserole, add the lamb and cook over a high heat until browned all over, stirring occasionally. Remove the meat from the casserole using a slotted spoon, then set aside and keep warm.

2 Reduce the heat slighty, then add the baby onions, crushed garlic and whole mushrooms to the oil remaining in the casserole and cook them gently for about 5 minutes, stirring occasionally with a wooden spoon.

3 Return the meat to the casserole, then add the dried apricots, stock, wine and tomato purée. Season to taste with salt and pepper and stir to mix.

4 Bring to the boil, stirring, then remove the casserole from the heat and cover. Transfer the casserole to the oven and cook for 1½–2 hours until the lamb is cooked and tender, stirring once or twice during the cooking time and adding a little extra stock, if necessary.

5 Meanwhile, make the dumplings. Place the flour, suet, herbs and seasoning in a bowl and stir to mix. Add enough cold water to make a soft, elastic dough. Divide the dough into small, marble-size pieces and, using lightly floured hands, roll each piece into a small ball.

6 Remove the lid from the casserole and place the dumplings on top of the braised lamb and vegetables.

7 Increase the oven temperature to 190°C/375°F/Gas 5. Return the casserole to the oven and cook for a further 20–25 minutes until the herb dumplings are cooked. Serve, garnished with the fresh herb sprigs.

VARIATIONS
Use lean beef or pork in place of the lamb and substitute shallots for the baby onions, if you prefer.

ROAST LAMB with BEANS and GREEN PEPPERCORNS

Roasting the lamb slowly on a bed of beans results in a dish that combines meltingly tender meat with vegetables all in one pot.

SERVES 6

8–10 garlic cloves, peeled
1.8–2kg/4–4½lb leg of lamb
30ml/2 tbsp olive oil
400g/14oz spinach leaves
400g/14oz can flageolet, cannellini or
    haricot (navy) beans, drained
400g/14oz can butter (lima) beans, drained
2 large, fresh rosemary sprigs, plus extra
    to garnish
15–30ml/1–2 tbsp drained, bottled
    green peppercorns

1 Preheat the oven to 150°C/300°F/ Gas 2. Set four garlic cloves aside and slice the rest lengthwise into three or four pieces. Make shallow slits in the skin of the lamb and insert a piece of garlic in each.

2 Heat the olive oil in a heavy, shallow flameproof casserole or a roasting pan that is large enough to hold the leg of lamb. Add the reserved garlic cloves and the fresh spinach leaves to the casserole or pan and cook over a medium heat, stirring occasionally, for 4–5 minutes, or until the spinach is wilted.

3 Add the beans and tuck the rosemary sprigs and peppercorns among them. Place the lamb on top, then cover the casserole or roasting pan with foil or a lid. Roast the lamb for 3–4 hours until it is cooked to your taste. Serve the lamb and beans hot, garnished with the remaining fresh rosemary sprigs.

MIDDLE-EASTERN ROAST LAMB and POTATOES

When the Eastern aroma of the garlic and saffron comes wafting out of the oven, this deliciously garlicky lamb won't last very long.

SERVES 6–8

2.75kg/6lb leg of lamb
4 garlic cloves, halved
60ml/4 tbsp olive oil
juice of I lemon
2–3 saffron threads, soaked in
   15ml/1 tbsp boiling water
5ml/1 tsp mixed dried herbs, oregano
   or marjoram
450g/1lb small baking potatoes,
   thickly sliced
2 large or 4 small onions,
   thickly sliced
salt and ground black pepper
fresh thyme, to garnish

1 Make eight evenly spaced incisions in the leg of lamb, press the halved garlic cloves into the slits and place the lamb in a large non-metallic dish.

2 Mix together the olive oil, lemon juice, saffron mixture and herbs. Rub over the lamb and marinate for 2 hours.

3 Preheat the oven to 180°C/350°F/ Gas 4. Layer the potato and onion slices in a large roasting pan. Lift the lamb out of the marinade and place it on top of the sliced potato and onions, fat side up and season well with plenty of salt and ground black pepper.

4 Pour the marinade over the lamb, then roast for 2 hours, basting occasionally. Remove from the oven and cover with foil, then rest for 10 minutes before carving. Garnish with thyme.

LAMB'S LIVER and BACON CASSEROLE

The trick when cooking liver is to seal it quickly, then simmer it gently and briefly.
Prolonged and/or fierce cooking makes liver hard and grainy. Boiled new potatoes
tossed in lots of butter go well with this simple casserole.

SERVES 4

30ml/2 tbsp extra virgin olive oil or
    sunflower oil
225g/8oz rindless unsmoked lean bacon
    rashers (strips), cut into pieces
2 onions, halved and sliced
175g/6oz/2 cups chestnut
    mushrooms, halved
450g/1lb lamb's liver, trimmed
    and sliced
25g/1oz/2 tbsp butter
15ml/1 tbsp soy sauce
30ml/2 tbsp plain (all-purpose) flour
150ml/¼ pint/⅔ cup hot, well-flavoured
    chicken stock
salt and ground black pepper

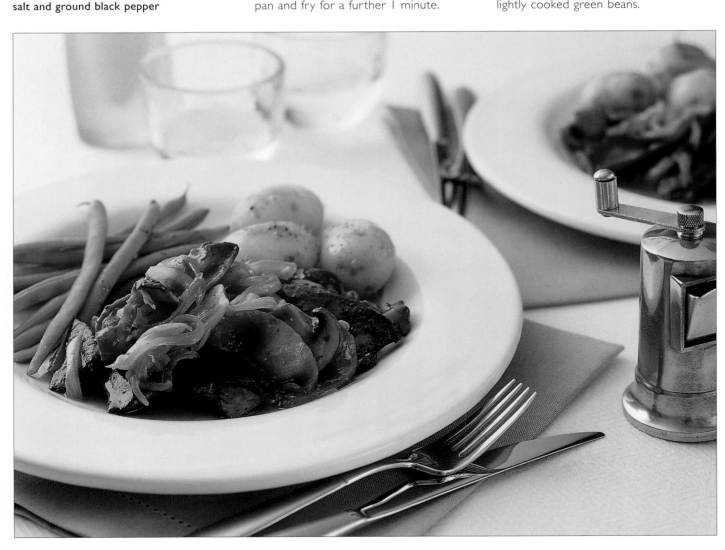

1 Heat the oil in a frying pan, add the bacon and fry until crisp. Add the sliced onions to the pan and cook for about 10 minutes, stirring frequently, or until softened. Add the mushrooms to the pan and fry for a further 1 minute.

2 Use a slotted spoon to remove the bacon and vegetables from the pan and keep warm. Add the liver to the fat remaining in the pan and cook over a high heat for 3–4 minutes, turning once to seal the slices on both sides. Remove the liver from the pan and keep warm.

3 Melt the butter in the pan, add the soy sauce and flour and blend together. Stir in the stock and bring to the boil, stirring until thickened. Return the liver, bacon and vegetables to the pan and heat through for 1 minute. Season with salt and pepper to taste, and serve immediately with new potatoes and lightly cooked green beans.

DEVILLED KIDNEYS on BRIOCHE CROÛTES

The expression "devilled" dates from the 18th century. It was used to describe dishes or foods that were seasoned with hot spices giving a fiery flavour that was associated with the devil and the heat of hell – in this case, cayenne pepper and Worcestershire sauce provide the "fire".

SERVES 4

8 mini brioche slices
25g/1oz/2 tbsp butter
1 shallot, finely chopped
2 garlic cloves, finely chopped
115g/4oz/1½ cups mushrooms, halved
1.5ml/¼ tsp cayenne pepper
15ml/1 tbsp Worcestershire sauce
8 lamb's kidneys, halved and trimmed
150ml/¼ pint/⅔ cup double (heavy) cream
30ml/2 tbsp chopped fresh parsley,
   to garnish

1 Preheat the grill (broiler) to high and toast the brioche slices until they are a golden brown colour on both sides, and keep warm.

2 Melt the butter in a large frying pan until it is just foaming. Add the finely chopped shallot, finely chopped garlic and halved mushrooms, then cook for about 5 minutes, or until the shallot is just beginning to soften. Stir in the cayenne pepper and the Worcestershire sauce and allow the mixture to simmer for about 1 minute, stirring continuously with a wooden spoon.

3 Add the kidneys to the pan and cook for 3–5 minutes on each side. Finally, stir in the cream and simmer for about 2 minutes, or until the sauce is heated through and slightly thickened.

4 Remove the brioche croûtes from the wire rack and place on warmed plates. Top with the kidneys. Sprinkle with the chopped parsley and serve immediately.

COOK'S TIPS
• If you can't find mini brioches, you can use a large brioche instead. Slice it thickly and stamp out croûtes using a 5cm/2in round cutter.
• If you prefer, the brioche croûtes can be fried rather than toasted. Melt 25g/1oz/ 2 tbsp butter in the frying pan and fry the croûtes until crisp and golden on both sides. Remove from the pan and drain on kitchen paper.

BEEF CARBONADE

This rich, dark stew of beef cooked slowly with lots of onions, garlic and beer is a classic casserole from the north of France and neighbouring Belgium.

SERVES 6

45ml/3 tbsp vegetable oil or beef dripping
3 onions, sliced
45ml/3 tbsp plain (all-purpose) flour
2.5ml/½ tsp mustard powder
1kg/2¼lb stewing beef (shin, shank or chuck), cut into large cubes
2–3 garlic cloves, finely chopped
300ml/½ pint/1¼ cups dark beer or ale
150ml/¼ pint/⅔ cup water
5ml/1 tsp dark brown sugar
1 fresh thyme sprig
1 fresh bay leaf
1 celery stick
salt and ground black pepper

For the topping
50g/2oz/¼ cup butter
1 garlic clove, crushed
15ml/1 tbsp Dijon mustard
45ml/3 tbsp chopped fresh parsley
6–12 slices of French baguette

1 Preheat the oven to 160°C/325°F/Gas 3. Heat 30ml/2 tbsp of the oil or dripping in a pan and cook the onions over a low heat until softened. Remove from the pan and set aside.

2 Meanwhile, mix together the flour and mustard and season. Toss the beef in the flour. Add the remaining oil or dripping to the pan and heat over a high heat. Brown the beef all over, then transfer it to a deep, earthenware baking dish.

3 Reduce the heat and return the onions to the pan. Add the garlic, cook briefly, then add the beer or ale, water and sugar. Tie the thyme and bay leaf together and add to the pan with the celery. Bring to the boil, stirring, then season with salt and pepper.

4 Pour the sauce over the beef and mix well. Cover tightly, then place in the oven and cook for 2½ hours. Check the beef once or twice to make sure that it is not too dry, adding a little extra water, if necessary. Test for tenderness, allowing an extra 30–40 minutes' cooking time if necessary.

5 To make the topping, beat together the butter, crushed garlic, Dijon mustard and 30ml/2 tbsp of the chopped fresh parsley. Spread the flavoured butter thickly over the bread. Increase the oven temperature to 190°C/375°F/Gas 5. Taste and season the stew, then arrange the prepared bread slices, buttered side uppermost, on top. Bake for 20 minutes, or until the bread is browned and crisp. Sprinkle the remaining chopped fresh parsley over the top to garnish and serve immediately.

BOEUF BOURGUIGNON

The classic French dish of beef cooked in Burgundy style, with red wine, small pieces of bacon, shallots and mushrooms, is baked for several hours at a low temperature.

SERVES 6

175g/6oz rindless streaky (fatty) bacon
   rashers (strips), chopped
900g/2lb lean braising steak, such as top
   rump (round) steak
30ml/2 tbsp plain (all-purpose) flour
45ml/3 tbsp sunflower oil
25g/1oz/2 tbsp butter
12 shallots
2 garlic cloves, crushed
175g/6oz/2⅓ cups mushrooms, sliced
450ml/¾ pint/scant 2 cups robust
   red wine
150ml/¼ pint/⅔ cup beef stock
   or consommé
1 bay leaf
2 sprigs each of fresh thyme, parsley
   and marjoram
salt and ground black pepper

1 Preheat the oven to 160°C/325°F/ Gas 3. Heat a large flameproof casserole, then add the bacon and cook, stirring occasionally, until the pieces are crisp and golden brown.

2 Meanwhile, cut the beef into 2.5cm/ 1in cubes. Season the flour and use to coat the meat. Use a slotted spoon to remove the bacon from the casserole and set aside. Add and heat the oil, then brown the beef in batches and set aside with the bacon.

COOK'S TIP
Beef consommé, which can be used as an alternative to beef stock in this recipe, is a clear, light soup. It is sold in cans, or in cartons as a fresh soup. Fresh beef stock is also available in cartons.

3 Add the butter to the fat remaining in the casserole. Cook the shallots and garlic until they are just beginning to colour, then add the mushrooms and cook for a further 5 minutes. Return the bacon and beef to the casserole, and stir in the wine and stock or consommé. Tie the herbs together into a bouquet garni and add to the casserole.

4 Cover and cook in the oven for 1½ hours, or until the meat is tender, stirring once or twice during the cooking time. Season to taste and serve the casserole with creamy mashed root vegetables, such as celeriac and potatoes.

COOK'S TIP
Boeuf Bourguignon freezes very well. Transfer the mixture to a dish so that it cools quickly, then pour it into a rigid plastic container. Push all the cubes of meat down into the sauce or they will dry out. Freeze for up to 2 months. Thaw overnight in the refrigerator, then transfer to a flameproof casserole and add 150ml/ ¼ pint/⅔ cup water. Stir well, then bring to the boil, stirring occasionally, and simmer steadily for at least 10 minutes, or until the meat is piping hot.

FILLET of BEEF STROGANOFF

Legend has it that this Russian recipe was devised by Count Paul Stroganov's cook to use beef frozen by the Siberian climate. The only way that it could be prepared was cut into very thin strips. The strips of lean beef were served in a brandy-flavoured cream sauce.

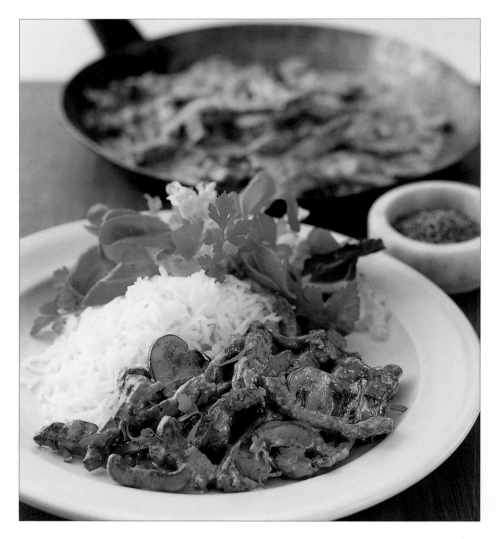

3 Cook the onion and garlic over a low heat, stirring occasionally until the onion has softened. Add the mushrooms and stir-fry over a high heat for 1–2 minutes. Transfer the vegetables and their juices to a dish and set aside.

4 Wipe the pan, then add and heat the remaining oil. Coat a batch of meat with flour, then fry over a high heat until well browned. Remove from the pan, then coat and fry another batch. When the last batch is cooked, replace all the meat and vegetables. Add the brandy and simmer until it has almost evaporated.

5 Stir in the beef stock or consommé and seasoning and cook for 10–15 minutes, stirring frequently with a wooden spoon, or until the meat is tender and the sauce is thick and glossy. Add the sour cream, stir well and sprinkle with the chopped fresh flat leaf parsley. Serve immediately with plain boiled rice and a simple salad.

COOK'S TIP
If you do not have a very large frying pan, it may be easier to cook this dish in a large, flameproof casserole.

SERVES 8

1.2kg/2½lb beef fillet (tenderloin)
30ml/2 tbsp plain (all-purpose) flour
large pinch each of cayenne pepper
    and paprika
75ml/5 tbsp sunflower oil
1 large onion, chopped
3 garlic cloves, finely chopped
450g/1lb/6½ cups chestnut
    mushrooms, sliced
75ml/5 tbsp brandy
300ml/½ pint/1¼ cups beef stock
    or consommé
300ml/½ pint/1¼ cups sour cream
45ml/3 tbsp chopped fresh flat leaf parsley
salt and ground black pepper

1 Thinly slice the beef fillet across the grain, then cut it into fine strips. Season the flour with the cayenne and paprika.

2 Heat half the oil in a large frying pan and add the chopped onion and garlic.

POT-ROAST BEEF with GUINNESS

This heart-warming, rich pot-roast is ideal for a winter supper. Brisket of beef has the best flavour but this dish works equally well with rolled silverside or topside.

SERVES 6

30ml/2 tbsp vegetable oil
900g/2lb rolled brisket of beef
275g/10oz onions, roughly chopped
2 celery sticks, thickly sliced
450g/1lb carrots, cut into large chunks
675g/1½lb potatoes, peeled and cut into
    large chunks
30ml/2 tbsp plain (all-purpose) flour
475ml/16fl oz/2 cups beef stock
300ml/½ pint/1¼ cups Guinness
1 bay leaf
45ml/3 tbsp chopped fresh thyme
5ml/1 tsp soft light brown sugar
30ml/2 tbsp wholegrain mustard
15ml/1 tbsp tomato purée (paste)
salt and ground black pepper

1 Preheat the oven to 180°C/350°F/ Gas 4. Heat the oil in a large flameproof casserole and brown the meat all over until golden.

3 Add the celery, carrot and potato to the casserole and cook over a medium heat for 2–3 minutes, or until they are just beginning to colour.

5 Add the bay leaf, thyme, sugar, mustard, tomato purée and plenty of seasoning. Place the meat on top, cover tightly and transfer to the oven.

2 Remove the meat from the pan and drain it on a double layer of kitchen paper. Add the chopped onions to the pan and cook for about 4 minutes, or until they are just beginning to soften and turn brown, stirring all the time.

4 Stir in the flour and cook for a further 1 minute stirring continuously. Pour in the beef stock and the Guinness and stir until well combined. Bring the sauce to the boil, stirring continuously with a wooden spoon.

6 Cook for about 2½ hours, or until the vegetables and meat are tender. Adjust the seasoning and add another pinch of sugar, if necessary. To serve, remove the meat and carve into thick slices. Serve with the vegetables and plenty of gravy.

CITRUS BEEF CURRY

This superbly aromatic Thai-style curry is not too hot but full of flavour. For a special meal, it goes perfectly with fried noodles.

SERVES 4

450g/1lb rump (round) steak
30ml/2 tbsp sunflower oil
30ml/2 tbsp medium curry paste
2 bay leaves
400ml/14fl oz/1⅔ cups coconut milk
300ml/½ pint/1¼ cups beef stock
30ml/2 tbsp lemon juice
45ml/3 tbsp Thai fish sauce
    (*nam pla*)
15ml/1 tbsp sugar
115g/4oz baby (pearl) onions, peeled but
    left whole
225g/8oz new potatoes, halved
115g/4oz/1 cup unsalted roasted peanuts,
    roughly chopped
115g/4oz fine green beans, halved
1 red (bell) pepper, seeded and
    thinly sliced
unsalted roasted peanuts, to
    garnish (optional)

1 Trim any fat off the beef and cut the beef into 5cm/2in strips.

2 Heat the sunflower oil in a large, heavy pan, add the curry paste and cook over a medium heat for 30 seconds, stirring constantly.

3 Add the beef and cook, stirring, for 2 minutes until it is beginning to brown and is thoroughly coated with the spices.

4 Stir in the bay leaves, coconut milk, stock, lemon juice, fish sauce and sugar, and bring to the boil, stirring.

5 Add the onions and potatoes, then bring back to the boil, reduce the heat and simmer, uncovered, for 5 minutes.

6 Stir in the peanuts, beans and pepper and simmer for a further 10 minutes, or until the beef and potatoes are tender. Serve in shallow bowls, with a spoon and fork, to enjoy all the rich and creamy juices. Sprinkle with extra unsalted roasted peanuts, if you like.

CALF'S LIVER with SLOW-COOKED ONIONS, MARSALA and SAGE

Liver and onions are an international favourite, from British liver with onion gravy to the famous Venetian dish of Fegato alla Veneziana. Inspired by Italian cooking, this dish is good served with polenta, either soft or set and grilled.

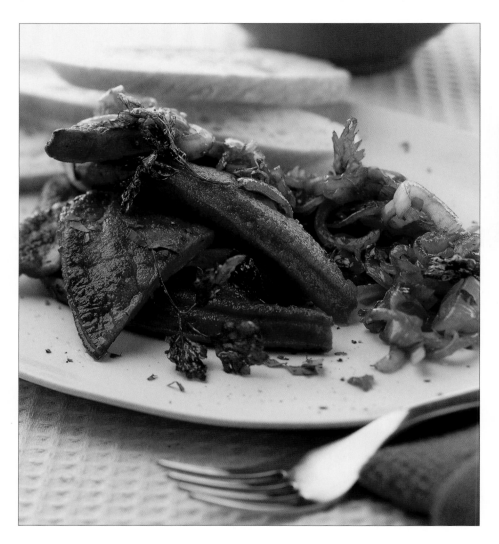

3 Add the remaining oil to the pan and fry the remaining sage leaves for about 30 seconds, then leave them to drain on kitchen paper.

4 Add the remaining butter and extra oil to the pan and increase the heat to high. Season the flour, then dip the liver in it and fry quickly for about 2 minutes on each side until browned, but still pink in the middle. Use a slotted spoon or metal spatula to transfer the liver to warm plates and keep warm.

5 Immediately add the Marsala to the pan and let it bubble fiercely until reduced to a few tablespoons of sticky glaze. Distribute the onions over the liver and spoon over the Marsala juices. Sprinkle with the fried sage leaves and extra parsley and serve immediately.

VARIATION

Chicken liver and onion bruschetta
Cook the onions as above, replacing the sage with 5ml/1 tsp chopped fresh thyme. Fry 400g/14oz chicken livers in 25g/1oz/ 2 tbsp butter and 15ml/1 tbsp olive oil until browned but still pink in the centre. Flame the chicken livers with 45ml/3 tbsp cognac, and add 150g/5oz seeded, skinned grapes (optional). Heat the grapes through, then toss them into the cooked onions. Heap the mixture on to thick slices of toasted country bread rubbed with oil and garlic or on to thick slices of grilled (broiled) polenta. Serve sprinkled with chopped fresh parsley.

SERVES 4

45ml/3 tbsp olive oil, plus extra for
   shallow frying
25g/1oz/2 tbsp butter
500g/1¼lb mild onions, thinly sliced
small bunch of fresh sage leaves
30ml/2 tbsp chopped fresh parsley, plus a
   little extra to garnish
2.5ml/½ tsp sugar
15ml/1 tbsp balsamic vinegar
30ml/2 tbsp plain (all-purpose) flour
675g/1½lb calf's liver, thinly sliced
150ml/¼ pint/⅔ cup Marsala
salt and ground black pepper

1 Heat half the oil with half the butter in a large, wide, heavy pan and cook the onions, covered, over a very gentle heat for 30 minutes. Stir once or twice.

2 Chop five of the sage leaves and add them to the pan with the chopped parsley, a pinch of salt, the sugar and balsamic vinegar. Cook, uncovered and stirring frequently with a wooden spoon, until the onions are very tender and a golden brown colour. Taste for seasoning and add salt and pepper as necessary. Tip the onions into a heatproof dish and keep warm.

BLACK BEAN CHILLI CON CARNE

Fresh green and dried red chillies add plenty of fire to this classic Tex-Mex dish of tender beef cooked in a spicy tomato sauce.

SERVES 6

225g/8oz/1¼ cups dried black beans
500g/1¼lb braising steak
30ml/2 tbsp vegetable oil
2 onions, chopped
1 garlic clove, crushed
1 fresh green chilli, seeded and
    finely chopped
15ml/1 tbsp paprika
10ml/2 tsp ground cumin
10ml/2 tsp ground coriander
400g/14oz can chopped tomatoes
300ml/½ pint/1¼ cups beef stock
1 dried red chilli, crumbled
5ml/1 tsp hot pepper sauce
1 fresh red (bell) pepper, seeded and chopped
salt
fresh coriander (cilantro), to garnish
boiled rice, to serve

1 Put the beans in a large pan. Add enough cold water to cover them, bring to the boil and boil vigorously for about 10 minutes. Drain, tip into a clean bowl, cover with cold water and leave to soak for about 8 hours or overnight.

2 Preheat the oven to 150°C/300°F/ Gas 2. Cut the braising steak into small dice. Heat the vegetable oil in a large, flameproof casserole. Add the chopped onion, crushed garlic and chopped green chilli and cook them gently for 5 minutes until soft, using a slotted spoon to transfer the mixture to a plate.

3 Increase the heat to high, add the meat to the casserole and brown on all sides, then stir in the paprika, ground cumin and ground coriander.

4 Add the tomatoes, beef stock, dried chilli and hot pepper sauce. Drain the beans and add them to the casserole, with enough water to cover. Bring to simmering point, cover and cook in the oven for 2 hours. Stir occasionally and add extra water, if necessary.

5 Season the casserole with salt and add the chopped red pepper. Replace the lid, return the casserole to the oven and cook for 30 minutes more, or until the meat and beans are tender. Sprinkle over the fresh coriander and serve with rice.

COOK'S TIP
Red kidney beans are traditionally used in chilli con carne, but in this recipe black beans are used instead. They are the same shape and size as red kidney beans but have a shiny black skin. They are also known as Mexican or Spanish black beans.

VARIATION
Use minced (ground) beef in place of the braising steak.

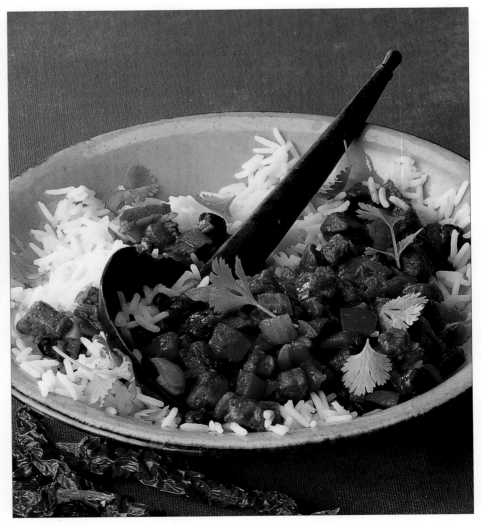

OSSO BUCCO with RISOTTO MILANESE

Two one-pot dishes in one recipe, both so utterly delicious that it seemed churlish to omit them from this collection. Osso Bucco is a traditional Milanese veal stew and is classically accompanied by this saffron-scented risotto.

SERVES 4

50g/2oz/¼ cup butter
15ml/1 tbsp olive oil
1 large onion, chopped
1 leek, finely chopped
45ml/3 tbsp plain (all-purpose) flour
4 large portions of veal shin, hind cut
600ml/1 pint/2½ cups dry white wine
salt and ground black pepper

For the risotto
25g/1oz/2 tbsp butter
1 onion, finely chopped
350g/12oz/1¾ cups risotto rice
1 litre/1¾ pints/4 cups chicken stock
2.5ml/½ tsp saffron threads
60ml/4 tbsp white wine
50g/2oz/⅔ cup freshly grated
    Parmesan cheese

For the gremolata
grated rind of 1 lemon
30ml/2 tbsp chopped fresh parsley
1 garlic clove, finely chopped

1 Heat the butter and oil until sizzling in a large heavy frying pan. Add the onion and leek, and cook gently for about 5 minutes. Season the flour and toss the veal in it, then add to the pan and cook over a high heat until it browns.

2 Gradually stir in the wine and heat until simmering. Cover the pan and simmer for 1½ hours, stirring occasionally. Use a slotted spoon to transfer the veal to a warmed serving dish, then boil the sauce over a high heat until it is reduced and thickened to the required consistency.

3 Make the risotto about 30 minutes before the end of the cooking time for the stew. Melt the butter in a large pan and cook the onion until softened.

4 Stir in the rice to coat all the grains in butter. Add a ladleful of boiling chicken stock and mix well. Continue adding the boiling stock a ladleful at a time, allowing each portion to be completely absorbed before adding the next.

5 Pound the saffron threads in a mortar, then stir in the wine. Add the saffron-scented wine to the risotto and cook for a final 5 minutes. Remove the pan from the heat and stir in the Parmesan.

6 Mix the lemon rind, chopped parsley and garlic together for the gremolata. Spoon some risotto on to each plate, then add some veal. Sprinkle each with a little gremolata and serve immediately.

SPICY VENISON CASSEROLE

Being low in fat but high in flavour, venison is an excellent choice for healthy, yet rich, casseroles. Cranberries and orange bring a festive fruitiness to this spicy recipe. Serve with small baked potatoes and green vegetables.

SERVES 4

15ml/1 tbsp olive oil
1 onion, chopped
2 celery sticks, sliced
10ml/2 tsp ground allspice
15ml/1 tbsp plain (all-purpose) flour
675g/1½lb stewing venison, cubed
225g/8oz fresh or frozen cranberries
grated rind and juice of 1 orange
900ml/1½ pints/3¾ cups beef or
    venison stock
salt and ground black pepper

1 Heat the oil in a flameproof casserole. Add the onion and celery and fry for about 5 minutes, or until softened.

2 Meanwhile, mix the ground allspice with the flour and either spread the mixture out on a large plate or place in a large plastic bag. Toss a few pieces of venison at a time (to prevent them becoming soggy) in the flour mixture until they are all lightly coated. Spread the floured venison out on a large plate until ready to cook.

3 When the onion and celery are just softened, remove them from the casserole using a slotted spoon and set aside. Add the venison pieces to the casserole in batches and cook until well browned and sealed on all sides.

COOK'S TIP
Freshly made stock is always best, but if you are short of time, look for cartons or tubs of fresh stock in the chilled food cabinets of large supermarkets.

4 Add the cranberries and the orange rind and juice to the casserole along with the stock, and stir well. Return the vegetables and the browned venison to the casserole and heat until simmering. Cover tightly and reduce the heat.

5 Simmer for about 45 minutes, or until the venison is tender, stirring occasionally. Season the venison casserole to taste with salt and pepper before serving.

VARIATIONS
Farmed venison is increasingly easy to find and is available from good butchers and many large supermarkets. It makes a rich and flavourful stew, but lean pork or braising steak could be used in place of the venison, if you prefer. You could also replace the cranberries with pitted and halved ready-to-eat prunes and, for extra flavour, use either ale or stout instead of about half the stock.

VENISON SAUSAGES with RED WINE GRAVY

Strongly flavoured, meaty sausages are delicious with a robust red wine gravy flavoured with assertive shiitake mushrooms. Serve with soft polenta, mashed potatoes or plenty of thickly sliced crusty bread to mop up the delicious gravy.

SERVES 4

15ml/1 tbsp sunflower oil (optional)
12 venison or wild boar sausages
2 leeks, sliced
2 plump garlic cloves, sliced
225g/8oz/3 cups shiitake
   mushrooms, quartered
15ml/1 tbsp plain (all-purpose) flour
600ml/1 pint/2½ cups red wine
30ml/2 tbsp chopped mixed fresh herbs,
   such as flat leaf parsley and marjoram
salt and ground black pepper

1 Pour the sunflower oil, if using, into a large frying pan, add the venison or wild boar sausages and cook over a medium heat for 15–20 minutes, turning frequently.

2 Add the leeks, garlic and mushrooms and mix well. Cook the vegetables for 10–15 minutes, or until the leeks are soft and beginning to brown.

3 Sprinkle in the flour and gradually pour in the red wine, stirring with a wooden spoon and pushing the sausages around to mix the flour and the liquid smoothly with the leeks.

4 Bring slowly to the boil, reduce the heat and simmer for 10–15 minutes, stirring occasionally, or until the gravy is smooth and glossy. Season the gravy with salt and pepper to taste and then sprinkle the mixed herbs over the sausages. Serve immediately with polenta or mashed potatoes.

COOK'S TIP
Shiitake mushrooms have a slightly floury-looking medium to dark grey-brown cap. They have a firm and meaty texture that becomes silky when cooked. The stalks can be tough so discard if necessary.

RABBIT with RED WINE and PRUNES

This is a favourite French dish and is often found on the menus of small country restaurants. It has a wonderfully rich flavour and the prunes add a delicious sweetness to the sauce. Serve with crisp, golden sautéed potatoes.

SERVES 4

8 rabbit portions
30ml/2 tbsp vegetable oil
2 onions, finely chopped
2 garlic cloves, finely chopped
60ml/4 tbsp Armagnac or brandy
300ml/½ pint/1¼ cups dry red wine
5ml/1 tsp soft light brown sugar
16 ready-to-eat prunes
150ml/¼ pint/⅔ cup double (heavy) cream
salt and ground black pepper

VARIATIONS

• Chicken can also be cooked in this way. Use 4 chicken drumsticks and 4 thighs in place of the rabbit portions.
• The prunes can be replaced with ready-to-eat dried apricots if you prefer – these go well with the rabbit and particularly well with chicken.

1 Season the rabbit portions liberally with salt and pepper. Heat the vegetable oil in a large, flameproof casserole and fry the rabbit portions in batches until they are golden brown on all sides.

2 Remove the browned rabbit portions from the casserole, add the chopped onion and garlic, and cook, stirring occasionally, until the onion is softened.

3 Return the rabbit to the casserole, add the Armagnac or brandy and ignite it. When the flames have died down, pour in the wine. Stir in the sugar and prunes, cover and simmer for 30 minutes.

4 Remove the rabbit from the casserole and keep warm. Add the cream to the sauce and simmer for 3–5 minutes, then season to taste and serve immediately.

OSTRICH STEW with SWEET POTATOES and CHICKPEAS

Lean and firm, ostrich meat marries well with the soft-textured sweet potatoes and chickpeas in this quick and easy, rich-flavoured stew.

SERVES 4

45ml/3 tbsp olive oil
1 large onion, chopped
2 garlic cloves, finely chopped
675g/1½lb ostrich fillet, cut into
  short strips
450g/1lb sweet potatoes, peeled
  and diced
2 × 400g/14oz cans chopped tomatoes
400g/14oz can chickpeas, drained
salt and ground black pepper
fresh oregano, to garnish

COOK'S TIP
Steamed couscous is a quick and easy accompaniment to this healthy stew, but it would also be good served with rice, or simply some warm, crusty bread.

1 Heat half the oil in a flameproof casserole. Add the chopped onion and garlic, and cook for about 5 minutes, or until softened but not coloured, stirring occasionally. Remove from the casserole using a slotted spoon and set aside. Add the remaining oil to the casserole and heat.

2 Fry the meat in batches over a high heat until browned. When the last batch is cooked, replace the meat and onions and stir in the potatoes, tomatoes and chickpeas. Bring to the boil, reduce the heat and simmer for 25 minutes, or until the meat is tender. Season and serve, garnished with the fresh oregano.

MARINATED PIGEON in RED WINE

The time taken to marinate and cook this casserole is well rewarded by the fabulous rich flavour of the finished dish. Stir-fried green cabbage and celeriac purée are delicious accompaniments to this casserole.

SERVES 4

4 pigeons (US squabs), about 225g/
   8oz each
30ml/2 tbsp olive oil
1 onion, coarsely chopped
225g/8oz/3¼ cups chestnut
   mushrooms, sliced
15ml/1 tbsp plain (all-purpose) flour
300ml/½ pint/1¼ cups game stock
30ml/2 tbsp chopped fresh parsley
salt and ground black pepper
flat leaf parsley, to garnish

For the marinade
15ml/1 tbsp light olive oil
1 onion, chopped
1 carrot, peeled and chopped
1 celery stick, chopped
3 garlic cloves, sliced
6 allspice berries, bruised
2 bay leaves
8 black peppercorns, bruised
150ml/¼ pint/⅔ cup red wine vinegar
150ml/¼ pint/⅔ cup red wine
45ml/3 tbsp redcurrant jelly

1 Mix together all the ingredients for the marinade in a large bowl. Add the pigeons and turn them in the marinade, then cover the bowl and chill for about 12 hours, turning the pigeons frequently.

VARIATIONS
If you are unable to buy pigeon, this recipe works equally well with chicken or rabbit. Buy portions and make deep slashes in the flesh so that the marinade soaks into, and flavours right to, the centre of the pieces of meat.

2 Preheat the oven to 150°C/300°F/ Gas 2. Heat the oil in a large, flameproof casserole and cook the onion and mushrooms for about 5 minutes, or until the onion has softened.

3 Meanwhile, drain the pigeons and strain the marinade into a jug (pitcher), then set both aside separately.

4 Sprinkle the flour over the pigeons and add them to the casserole, breast-sides down. Pour in the marinade and stock, and add the chopped parsley and seasoning. Cover and cook for 2½ hours.

5 Check the seasoning, then serve the pigeons on warmed plates and ladle the sauce over them. Garnish with parsley.

GROUSE with ORCHARD FRUIT STUFFING

Tart apples, plums and pears make a fabulous orchard fruit stuffing that complements the rich gamey flavour of grouse perfectly.

SERVES 2

juice of ½ lemon
2 young grouse
50g/2oz/¼ cup butter
4 Swiss chard leaves
50ml/2fl oz/¼ cup Marsala
salt and ground black pepper

For the stuffing
2 shallots, finely chopped
1 tart cooking apple, peeled, cored
   and chopped
1 pear, peeled, cored and chopped
2 plums, halved, stoned (pitted)
   and chopped
large pinch of mixed (apple pie) spice

1 Sprinkle the lemon juice over the grouse and season well. Melt half the butter in a flameproof casserole, add the grouse and cook for 10 minutes, or until browned. Use tongs to remove the grouse from the casserole and set aside.

2 Add the shallots to the fat remaining in the casserole and cook until softened but not coloured. Add the apple, pear, plums and mixed spice, and cook for about 5 minutes, or until the fruits are just beginning to soften. Remove the casserole from the heat and spoon the hot fruit mixture into the body cavities of the birds.

3 Truss the birds neatly with string. Smear the remaining butter over the birds and wrap them in the chard leaves, then replace them in the casserole.

4 Pour in the Marsala and heat until simmering. Cover tightly and simmer for 20 minutes, or until the birds are tender, taking care not to overcook them. Leave to rest in a warm place for about 10 minutes before serving.

COOK'S TIP
There isn't a lot of liquid in the casserole for cooking the birds – they are steamed rather than boiled, so it is very important that the casserole has a heavy base and a tight-fitting lid, otherwise the liquid may evaporate and the chard will burn on the base of the pan.

BRAISED PHEASANT with WILD MUSHROOMS, CHESTNUTS and BACON

Pheasant at the end of their season are not suitable for roasting, so consider this tasty casserole enriched with wild mushrooms and chestnuts. Allow two birds for four people.

SERVES 4

2 mature pheasants
50g/2oz/¼ cup butter
75ml/5 tbsp brandy
12 baby (pearl) onions, peeled
1 celery stick, chopped
50g/2oz unsmoked rindless bacon,
   cut into strips
45ml/3 tbsp plain (all-purpose) flour
550ml/18fl oz/2¼ cups chicken
   stock, boiling
175g/6oz peeled, cooked chestnuts
350g/12oz/4 cups fresh ceps, trimmed and
   sliced, or 15g/½oz/¼ cup dried porcini
   mushrooms, soaked in warm water for
   20 minutes
15ml/1 tbsp lemon juice
salt and ground black pepper
watercress sprigs, to garnish

2 Wipe out the casserole and melt the remaining butter. Add the onions, celery and bacon and brown lightly. Stir in the flour. Remove from the heat.

3 Stir in the stock gradually so that it is completely absorbed by the flour. Add the chestnuts, mushrooms, the pheasants and their juices. Bring back to a gentle simmer, then cover and cook in the oven for 1½ hours.

4 Transfer the cooked pheasants and vegetables to a warmed serving plate. Bring the sauce back to the boil, add the lemon juice and season to taste. Pour the sauce into a jug (pitcher) or gravy boat and garnish the birds with watercress.

COOK'S TIP
Cooking and peeling fresh chestnuts can be hard work, so look out for ready-peeled canned or vacuum-packed varieties.

1 Preheat the oven to 160°C/325°F/ Gas 3. Season the pheasants with salt and pepper. Melt half of the butter in a large flameproof casserole and brown the pheasants over a medium heat. Transfer the pheasants to a shallow dish and pour off the cooking fat. Return the casserole to the heat and brown the sediment. Add the brandy, stir well to loosen the sediment using a flat wooden spoon, then pour all the cooking juices over the pheasant.

COOK'S TIP
When buying pheasant choose birds that look fresh. They should be plump and firm, with supple skin. Game birds have a strong odour but they should never smell unpleasant or "off".

CHICKEN AND POULTRY MAIN MEALS

Chicken and duck are perfect ingredients for cooking in one pot and there is nothing better than succulent poultry that has been cooked in the same pot as fresh herbs and vegetables or rice. For an unforgettable taste sensation, you could try mouthwatering Mediterranean Duck with Harissa and Saffron or Chicken Baked with Shallots, Garlic and Fennel. Equally delicious are those dishes that include rice such as Chicken and Prawn Jambalaya, or creamy Risotto with Chicken.

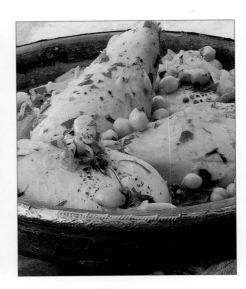

CHICKEN CASSEROLE with WINTER VEGETABLES

A casserole of wonderfully tender chicken, root vegetables and lentils, finished with crème fraîche, mustard and tarragon.

SERVES 4

350g/12oz onions
350g/12oz leeks
225g/8oz carrots
450g/1lb swede (rutabaga)
30ml/2 tbsp oil
4 chicken portions, about 900g/2lb
    total weight
115g/4oz/½ cup green lentils
475ml/16fl oz/2 cups chicken stock
300ml/½ pint/1¼ cups apple juice
10ml/2 tsp cornflour (cornstarch)
45ml/3 tbsp crème fraîche
10ml/2 tsp wholegrain mustard
30ml/2 tbsp chopped fresh tarragon
salt and ground black pepper
fresh tarragon sprigs, to garnish

1 Preheat the oven to 190°C/375°F/ Gas 5. Prepare the onions, leeks, carrots and swede and roughly chop them.

COOK'S TIP
Chop the vegetables into similarly sized pieces so that they cook evenly.

2 Heat the oil in a large flameproof casserole. Season the chicken portions with plenty of salt and pepper and brown them in the hot oil until golden. Drain on kitchen paper.

3 Add the onions to the casserole and cook for 5 minutes, stirring, until they begin to soften and colour. Add the leeks, carrots, swede and lentils to the casserole and stir over a medium heat for 2 minutes.

4 Return the chicken to the pan, then add the stock, apple juice and seasoning. Bring to the boil and cover tightly. Cook in the oven for 50–60 minutes, or until the chicken and lentils are tender.

5 Place the casserole on the stove-top over a medium heat. In a small bowl, blend the cornflour with about 30ml/ 2 tbsp water to make a smooth paste and add to the casserole with the crème fraîche, wholegrain mustard and chopped tarragon. Adjust the seasoning, then simmer gently for about 2 minutes, stirring, until thickened slightly, before serving, garnished with tarragon sprigs.

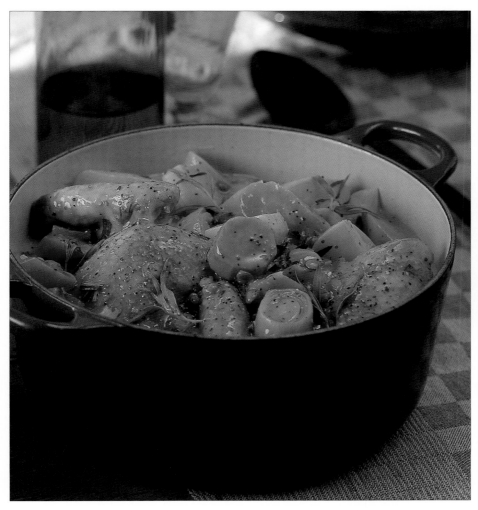

COQ au VIN

This French country casserole was traditionally made with an old boiling bird, marinated overnight in red wine, then simmered gently until tender. Modern recipes use tender roasting birds to save time and because boiling fowl are not readily available.

SERVES 6

45ml/3 tbsp light olive oil
12 shallots
225g/8oz rindless streaky (fatty) bacon
    rashers (strips), chopped
3 garlic cloves, finely chopped
225g/8oz small mushrooms, halved
6 boneless chicken thighs
3 boneless chicken breast
    portions, halved
1 bottle red wine
salt and ground black pepper
45ml/3 tbsp chopped fresh parsley,
    to garnish

For the bouquet garni
3 sprigs each parsley, thyme and sage
1 bay leaf
4 peppercorns

For the beurre manié
25g/1oz/2 tbsp butter, softened
25g/1oz/¼ cup plain (all-purpose) flour

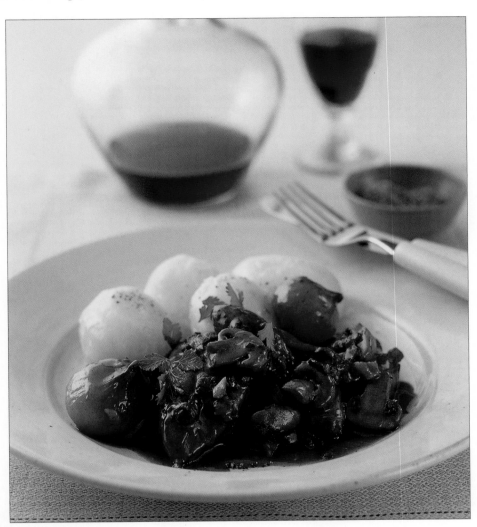

1 Heat the oil in a large, flameproof casserole and cook the shallots for about 5 minutes, or until golden. Increase the heat, then add the chopped bacon, garlic and mushrooms and cook for a further 10 minutes, stirring frequently.

2 Use a slotted spoon to transfer the cooked ingredients to a plate, then brown the chicken portions in the oil remaining in the pan, turning them until they are golden brown all over. Return the cooked shallots, garlic, mushrooms and bacon to the casserole and pour in the red wine.

3 Tie the ingredients for the bouquet garni in a bundle in a small piece of muslin (cheesecloth) and add to the casserole. Bring to the boil, reduce the heat and cover the casserole with a tightly fitting lid, then simmer for 30–40 minutes.

4 To make the beurre manié, cream the butter and flour together in a small bowl using your fingers or a spoon to make a smooth paste.

5 Add small lumps of the beurre manié paste to the bubbling casserole, stirring well until each piece has melted into the liquid before adding the next. When all the paste has been added, bring the casserole back to the boil and simmer for 5 minutes.

6 Season the casserole to taste with salt and pepper and serve garnished with chopped fresh parsley and accompanied by boiled potatoes.

HUNTER'S CHICKEN

This traditional dish sometimes has strips of green pepper in the sauce instead of the mushrooms. Creamed potato or polenta makes a good accompaniment.

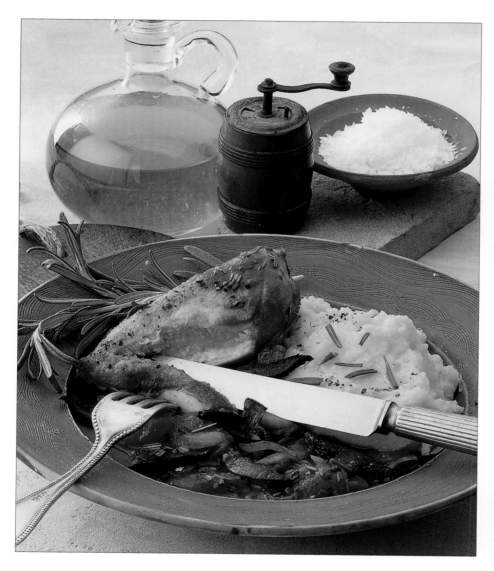

SERVES 4

15g/½oz/¼ cup dried porcini mushrooms
30ml/2 tbsp olive oil
15g/½oz/1 tbsp butter
4 chicken portions, on the bone, skinned
1 large onion, thinly sliced
400g/14oz can chopped tomatoes
150ml/¼ pint/⅔ cup red wine
1 garlic clove, crushed
leaves of 1 fresh rosemary sprg,
    finely chopped
115g/4oz/1¾ cups fresh field (portabello)
    mushrooms, thinly sliced
salt and ground black pepper
fresh rosemary sprigs, to garnish

1 Put the porcini in a bowl, add 250ml/
8fl oz/1 cup warm water and soak for
20 minutes. Squeeze the porcini over
the bowl, strain the liquid and reserve.
Finely chop the porcini.

2 Heat the oil and butter in a large,
flameproof casserole until foaming. Add
the chicken portions and sauté over a
medium heat for 5 minutes, or until
golden brown. Remove the pieces and
drain on kitchen paper.

3 Add the sliced onion and chopped
porcini mushrooms to the pan. Cook
gently, stirring frequently, for about
3 minutes until the onion has softened
but not browned. Stir in the chopped
tomatoes, red wine and reserved
mushroom soaking liquid, then add the
crushed garlic and chopped rosemary,
with salt and pepper to taste. Bring to
the boil, stirring constantly.

4 Return the chicken to the casserole
and turn to coat with the sauce. Cover
with a tightly fitting lid and simmer gently
for 30 minutes.

5 Add the fresh mushrooms to the
casserole and stir well to mix into the
sauce. Continue simmering gently for
10 minutes, or until the chicken is
tender. Taste for seasoning. Serve hot,
with creamed potato or polenta, if you
like. Garnish with the rosemary sprigs.

SEVILLE CHICKEN

Oranges and almonds are favourite ingredients in southern Spain, especially around Seville, where the orange and almond trees are a familiar and wonderful sight.

SERVES 4

1 orange
8 chicken thighs
plain (all-purpose) flour, seasoned with salt
    and pepper
45ml/3 tbsp olive oil
1 large Spanish onion, roughly chopped
2 garlic cloves, crushed
1 red (bell) pepper, seeded and sliced
1 yellow (bell) pepper, seeded
    and sliced
115g/4oz chorizo, sliced
50g/2oz/½ cup flaked (sliced) almonds
225g/8oz/generous 1 cup brown
    basmati rice
about 600ml/1 pint/2½ cups chicken or
    vegetable stock
400g/14oz can chopped tomatoes
175ml/6fl oz/¾ cup white wine
generous pinch of dried thyme
salt and ground black pepper
fresh thyme sprigs, to garnish

1 Pare a thin strip of peel from the orange using a vegetable peeler and set it aside. Peel the orange, then cut it into even segments, working over a bowl to catch any excess juice. Dust the chicken thighs with plenty of seasoned flour.

2 Heat the olive oil in a large frying pan and fry the chicken pieces on both sides until nicely brown. Transfer the browned chicken to a plate. Add the chopped onion and crushed garlic to the pan and fry for 4–5 minutes until the onion begins to brown. Add the sliced red and yellow peppers to the pan and fry, stirring occasionally with a wooden spoon, until they are slightly softened.

3 Add the chorizo, stir-fry for a few minutes, then sprinkle over the almonds and rice. Cook, stirring, for 1–2 minutes.

4 Pour in the chicken or vegetable stock, chopped tomatoes and white wine, then add the reserved orange peel and the dried thyme. Season well. Bring the sauce to simmering point, stirring, then return the chicken to the pan.

5 Cover tightly and cook over a very low heat for 1–1¼ hours until the rice and chicken are tender. Just before serving, add the orange segments and juice, and allow to cook briefly to heat through. Season to taste, garnish with sprigs of fresh thyme and serve.

CHICKEN BAKED with SHALLOTS, GARLIC and FENNEL

This is a very simple and delicious way to cook chicken. If you have time, leave the chicken to marinate for a few hours for the best flavour.

SERVES 4

1.6–1.8kg/3½–4lb chicken, cut into
    8 pieces, or 8 chicken joints
250g/9oz shallots, peeled
1 head of garlic, separated into cloves
    and peeled
60ml/4 tbsp extra virgin olive oil
45ml/3 tbsp tarragon vinegar
45ml/3 tbsp white wine or
    vermouth (optional)
5ml/1 tsp fennel seeds, crushed
2 bulbs fennel, cut into wedges, feathery
    tops reserved
150ml/¼ pint/⅔ cup double (heavy) cream
5ml/1 tsp redcurrant jelly
15ml/1 tbsp tarragon mustard
a little sugar (optional)
30ml/2 tbsp chopped fresh flat leaf parsley
salt and ground black pepper

1 Place the chicken pieces, shallots and all but one of the garlic cloves in a large, shallow flameproof dish. Add the olive oil, tarragon vinegar, white wine or vermouth, if using, and the crushed fennel seeds. Season to taste with plenty of ground black pepper, then set aside and leave to marinate in a cool place for 2–3 hours.

2 Preheat the oven to 190°C/375°F/Gas 5. Add the wedges of fennel to the chicken, then season with salt and stir well to mix. Transfer the chicken to the oven and cook for 50–60 minutes, stirring once or twice, until the chicken is thoroughly cooked. The chicken juices should run clear, not pink, when the thick thigh meat is pierced with a skewer or a small sharp knife.

3 Transfer the chicken and vegetables to a serving dish and keep them warm. Skim off some of the fat and bring the cooking juices to the boil, then pour in the cream. Stir, scraping up all the juices. Whisk in the redcurrant jelly followed by the mustard. Check the seasoning, adding a little sugar, if necessary.

4 Finely chop the remaining garlic clove with the feathery fennel tops and mix them with the parsley. Pour the sauce over the chicken and then sprinkle the chopped garlic and herb mixture over the top. Serve immediately with rice or baked potatoes.

COOK'S TIPS
• If possible, use the fresh, new season's garlic for this dish, as it is plump, moist and full of flavour. Purple-skinned garlic is considered by many cooks to have the best flavour.
• The cut surfaces of fennel will quickly discolour, so do not prepare it too far in advance of using it. If you must prepare it beforehand, then put the wedges into a bowl of cold water acidulated with a little lemon juice.

CHICKEN with FORTY CLOVES of GARLIC

This dish does not have to be mathematically exact, so do not worry if you have 35 or even 50 cloves of garlic — the important thing is that there should be lots. The smell that emanates from the oven as the chicken and garlic cook is indescribably delicious.

SERVES 4–5

5–6 whole heads of garlic
15g/½oz/1 tbsp butter
45ml/3 tbsp olive oil
1.8–2kg/4–4½lb chicken
150g/5oz/1¼ cups plain (all-purpose) flour,
    plus 5ml/1 tsp
75ml/5 tbsp white port, Pineau
    de Charentes or other white,
    fortified wine
2–3 fresh tarragon or rosemary sprigs
30ml/2 tbsp crème fraîche (optional)
a few drops of lemon juice (optional)
salt and ground black pepper

1 Separate three of the heads of garlic into cloves and peel them. Remove the first layer of papery skin from the remaining heads of garlic and cut off the tops to expose the cloves, if you like, or leave them whole. Preheat the oven to 180°C/350°F/Gas 4.

2 Heat the butter and 15ml/1 tbsp of the olive oil in a flameproof casserole that is just large enough to take the chicken and garlic. Add the chicken and cook over a medium heat, turning it frequently, for 10–15 minutes, until it is browned all over.

3 Sprinkle in 5ml/1 tsp flour and cook for 1 minute. Add the port or wine. Tuck in the whole heads of garlic and the peeled cloves with the sprigs of tarragon or rosemary. Pour over the remaining oil and season to taste with salt and pepper.

4 Mix the main batch of flour with sufficient water to make a firm dough. Roll it out into a long sausage and press it around the rim of the casserole, then press on the lid, folding the dough up and over it to create a tight seal. Cook in the oven for 1½ hours.

5 To serve, lift off the lid to break the seal and remove the chicken and whole garlic to a serving platter and keep warm. Remove and discard the herb sprigs, then place the casserole on the stove top and whisk the remaining ingredients to combine the garlic cloves with the juices. Add the crème fraîche, if using, and a little lemon juice to taste, if using. Process the sauce in a food processor or blender until smooth. Reheat the garlic sauce in a clean pan if necessary and serve it with the chicken.

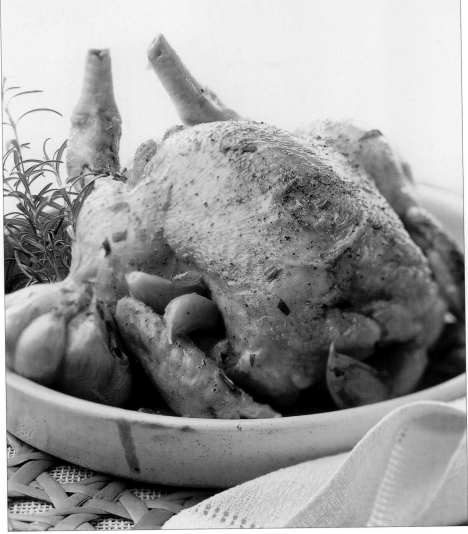

CHICKEN with CHICKPEAS and ALMONDS

The almonds in this tasty Moroccan-style recipe are pre-cooked until soft, adding an interesting texture and flavour to the chicken.

SERVES 4

75g/3oz/½ cup blanched almonds
75g/3oz/½ cup chickpeas, soaked overnight
   and drained
4 part-boned chicken breast portions, skinned
50g/2oz/4 tbsp butter
2.5ml/½ tsp saffron threads
2 Spanish onions, finely sliced
900ml/1½ pints/3¾ cups chicken stock
1 small cinnamon stick
60ml/4 tbsp chopped fresh flat leaf
   parsley, plus extra to garnish
lemon juice, to taste
salt and ground black pepper

1 Place the blanched almonds and the soaked and drained chickpeas in a large flameproof casserole of water and bring to the boil. Boil for 10 minutes, then reduce the heat. Simmer for 1–1½ hours until the chickpeas are soft. Drain the chickpeas and almonds and set aside.

2 Place the skinned chicken pieces in the casserole, together with the butter, half of the saffron, and salt and plenty of black pepper. Heat gently, stirring, until the butter has melted.

3 Add the onions and stock, bring to the boil, then add the reserved cooked almonds, chickpeas and cinnamon stick. Cover with a tightly fitting lid and cook very gently for 45–60 minutes until the chicken is completely tender.

4 Transfer the cooked chicken to a serving plate and keep warm. Bring the sauce to the boil and cook over a high heat until it is well reduced, stirring frequently with a wooden spoon.

5 Add the chopped parsley and remaining saffron to the casserole and cook for a further 2–3 minutes. Sharpen the sauce with a little lemon juice, then pour the sauce over the chicken and serve, garnished with extra fresh parsley.

CHICKEN with TOMATOES and HONEY

A thick tomato and honey sauce coats chicken pieces in this subtly spiced dish.

SERVES 4

30ml/2 tbsp sunflower oil
25g/1oz/2 tbsp butter
4 chicken quarters
1 onion, grated or very finely chopped
1 garlic clove, crushed
5ml/1 tsp ground cinnamon
good pinch of ground ginger
1.3–1.6kg/3–3½lb tomatoes, peeled,
   cored and roughly chopped
30ml/2 tbsp clear honey
50g/2oz/⅓ cup blanched almonds
15ml/1 tbsp sesame seeds
salt and ground black pepper
chopped flat leaf parsley, to garnish

1 Place the oil and butter in a large, flameproof casserole. Add the chicken and cook over a medium heat for about 3 minutes until it is lightly browned.

2 Add the grated or chopped onion, garlic, cinnamon, ginger, tomatoes and plenty of seasoning, and heat gently until the tomatoes begin to bubble.

3 Lower the heat and then cover the casserole. Simmer very gently for about 1 hour, stirring and turning the chicken occasionally, or until it is completely cooked through.

4 Lift out the chicken pieces and transfer them to a plate. Increase the heat and cook the tomato sauce until it is reduced to a thick purée, stirring frequently. Stir in the honey, cook for 1 minute, then return the chicken pieces to the pan and cook for 2–3 minutes to heat through.

5 Transfer the chicken and sauce to a warmed serving dish and sprinkle with the blanched almonds and sesame seeds. Serve hot, garnished with parsley.

COOK'S TIP

To blanch whole almonds, place them in a strainer and lower it into boiling water. Cook the almonds for 2–3 minutes, then remove the strainer from the water. Pinch the softened almond skin between your thumb and finger to squeeze it off.

OVEN-ROASTED CHICKEN with MEDITERRANEAN VEGETABLES

This is a delicious – and trouble-free – alternative to a traditional roast chicken. The recipe also works very well with guinea fowl.

SERVES 4

1.8–2.25kg/4–5lb roasting chicken
150ml/¼ pint/⅔ cup extra virgin olive oil
½ lemon
a few sprigs of fresh thyme
450g/1lb small new potatoes
1 aubergine (eggplant), cut into
   2.5cm/1in cubes
1 red or yellow (bell) pepper, seeded
   and quartered
1 fennel bulb, trimmed and quartered
8 large garlic cloves, unpeeled
coarse salt and ground black pepper

1 Preheat the oven to 200°C/400°F/ Gas 6. Rub the chicken all over with olive oil and season with pepper. Place the lemon half inside the bird, with a sprig or two of thyme. Put the chicken breast side down in a large roasting pan. Roast for about 30 minutes.

2 Remove the chicken from the oven and season with salt. Turn the chicken right side up, and baste with the juices from the pan.

3 Arrange the potatoes around the chicken and roll them in the cooking juices until they are thoroughly coated. Return the roasting pan to the oven, to continue roasting.

4 After 30 minutes, add the aubergine, red pepper, fennel and garlic cloves to the pan. Drizzle the vegetables with the remaining oil, and season to taste with salt and pepper.

5 Add the remaining sprigs of thyme to the roasting pan, tucking the sprigs in among the vegetables. Return the chicken and vegetables to the oven and cook for 30–50 minutes more, basting and turning the vegetables occasionally during cooking.

6 To find out if the chicken is cooked, push the tip of a small sharp knife between the thigh and breast – if the juices run clear, rather than pink, it is done. The vegetables should be tender and beginning to brown. Serve the chicken and vegetables from the pan.

CHICKEN PIRI-PIRI

This is a classic Portuguese dish, based on a hot sauce made from Angolan chillies. It is popular wherever there are Portuguese communities, and is often served in South Africa.

SERVES 4

4 chicken breast portions
30–45ml/2–3 tbsp olive oil
1 large onion, finely sliced
2 carrots, cut into thin strips
1 large parsnip or 2 small parsnips,
    cut into thin strips
1 red (bell) pepper, seeded and sliced
1 yellow (bell) pepper, seeded
    and sliced
1 litre/1¾ pints/4 cups chicken or
    vegetable stock
3 tomatoes, peeled, seeded and chopped
generous dash of piri-piri sauce
15ml/1 tbsp tomato purée (paste)
½ cinnamon stick
1 fresh thyme sprig, plus extra fresh thyme
    to garnish
1 bay leaf
275g/10oz/1½ cups white long grain rice
15ml/1 tbsp lime or lemon juice
salt and ground black pepper

1 Preheat the oven to 180°C/350°F/ Gas 4. Rub the chicken skin with a little salt and ground black pepper. Heat 30ml/2 tbsp of the olive oil in a large frying pan, add the chicken portions and cook, turning occasionally until browned on all sides. Transfer to a plate using a fish slice (spatula).

2 Add some more oil to the pan if necessary, add the sliced onion and fry for 2–3 minutes until slightly softened. Add the carrot and parsnip strips and the pepper slices and stir-fry for a few minutes more. Cover the pan and cook for 4–5 minutes until all the vegetables are quite soft.

3 Pour in the chicken or vegetable stock, then add the tomatoes, piri-piri sauce, tomato purée and cinnamon stick. Stir in the thyme and bay leaf. Season to taste and bring to the boil. Using a ladle, spoon off 300ml/½ pint/1¼ cups of the liquid and set aside in a small pan.

4 Put the rice in the base of a large earthenware dish. Using a slotted spoon, scoop the vegetables out of the frying pan and spread them over the rice. Arrange the chicken pieces on top. Pour over the spicy chicken stock from the frying pan, cover tightly and cook in the oven for about 45 minutes, until both the rice and chicken are completely tender.

5 Meanwhile, heat the reserved chicken stock, adding a few more drops of piri-piri sauce and the lime or lemon juice.

6 To serve, spoon the piri-piri chicken and rice on to warmed serving plates. Serve the remaining sauce separately or poured over the chicken.

CHICKEN BIRIANI

Easy to make and very tasty, this is the ideal one-pot dish for a family supper.

SERVES 4

10 green cardamom pods
275g/10oz/1½ cups basmati rice, soaked
    and drained
2.5ml/½ tsp salt
2–3 cloves
5cm/2in cinnamon stick
45ml/3 tbsp vegetable oil
3 onions, sliced
4 chicken breast portions, each about
    175g/6oz, cubed
1.5ml/¼ tsp ground cloves
5ml/1 tsp ground cumin
5ml/1 tsp ground coriander
2.5ml/½ tsp ground black pepper
3 garlic cloves, chopped
5ml/1 tsp finely chopped fresh root ginger
juice of 1 lemon
4 tomatoes, sliced
30ml/2 tbsp chopped fresh
    coriander (cilantro)
150ml/¼ pint/⅔ cup natural (plain) yogurt
4–5 saffron threads, soaked in 10ml/2 tsp
    hot milk
150ml/¼ pint/⅔ cup water
toasted flaked (sliced) almonds and fresh
    coriander (cilantro) sprigs, to garnish
natural (plain) yogurt, to serve

1 Preheat the oven to 190°C/375°F/
Gas 5. Remove the seeds from half the
cardamom pods and grind them finely, using
a mortar and pestle. Set the seeds aside.

2 Bring a flameproof casserole of water
to the boil and add the soaked and
drained basmati rice, then stir in the salt,
the remaining whole cardamom pods,
whole cloves and cinnamon stick. Boil
the rice for 2 minutes, then drain,
leaving the whole spices in the rice.

3 Heat the oil in the flameproof
casserole and fry the onions for about
8 minutes, until softened and browned.
Add the cubed chicken and the ground
spices, including the ground cardamom
seeds. Mix well, then add the chopped
garlic, ginger and lemon juice. Stir-fry the
mixture together for 5 minutes.

4 Arrange the sliced tomatoes on top.
Sprinkle on the coriander, spoon the
yogurt on top and cover with the rice.

5 Drizzle the saffron milk over the rice
and add the water. Cover and bake for
1 hour. Garnish with almonds and
coriander and serve with extra yogurt.

CHICKEN and PRAWN JAMBALAYA

This colourful mixture of rice, peppers and tomatoes with chicken, gammon and prawns is flavoured with garlic and fresh herbs and a few dashes of fiery Tabasco sauce. It's an ideal dish for big family gatherings and celebrations.

SERVES 10

2 chickens, each about 1.3–1.6kg/3–3½lb
450g/1lb piece raw smoked gammon
   (smoked or cured ham)
50g/2oz/⅓ cup lard or
   bacon fat
50g/2oz/½ cup plain (all-purpose) flour
3 onions, finely sliced
2 green (bell) peppers, seeded and sliced
675g/1½lb tomatoes, peeled and chopped
2–3 garlic cloves, crushed
10ml/2 tsp chopped fresh thyme or
   5ml/1 tsp dried thyme
24 raw Mediterranean prawns (jumbo
   shrimp), peeled with tails intact
500g/1¼lb/2½ cups white long grain rice
1.2 litres/2 pints/5 cups water
2–3 dashes Tabasco sauce
45ml/3 tbsp chopped fresh flat leaf parsley,
   plus tiny fresh parsley sprigs to garnish
salt and ground black pepper

4 Add the diced gammon, onions, green peppers, tomatoes, garlic and thyme and stir well to mix. Cook, stirring regularly, for about 10 minutes, then add the prawns and mix lightly.

5 Stir the rice into the frying pan and pour in the water. Season well with salt, black pepper and Tabasco sauce. Bring to the boil, then cook gently, stirring occasionally, until the rice is tender and all the liquid has been fully absorbed. Add a little extra boiling water if the rice looks like drying out before it is cooked. Check the seasoning and add salt, pepper and more Tabasco if necessary.

6 Mix the chopped fresh flat leaf parsley into the finished dish, garnish with tiny sprigs of flat leaf parsley and serve the jambalaya immediately with plenty of crusty bread.

1 Cut each chicken into ten pieces and season the pieces well with salt and pepper. Dice the gammon, discarding the rind and fat.

2 Melt the lard or bacon fat in a large, heavy frying pan. Add the chicken pieces in several batches, cook them until they are golden brown all over, then lift them out with a slotted spoon and set them aside.

3 Reduce the heat. Sprinkle the flour into the fat in the pan and stir with a wooden spoon until the roux turns a golden brown colour. Return the chicken pieces to the pan.

RISOTTO with CHICKEN

This is a classic risotto combination of creamy rice and tender cubes of chicken, flavoured with aromatic saffron, prosciutto, white wine and Parmesan cheese.

SERVES 6

30ml/2 tbsp olive oil
225g/8oz skinless, boneless chicken breast
    portions, cut into 2.5cm/1in cubes
1 onion, finely chopped
1 garlic clove, finely chopped
450g/1lb/2¼ cups risotto rice
120ml/4fl oz/½ cup dry white wine
1.5ml/¼ tsp saffron threads
1.75 litres/3 pints/7½ cups simmering
    chicken stock
50g/2oz prosciutto, cut into
    thin strips
25g/1oz/2 tbsp butter, diced
25g/1oz/⅓ cup freshly grated Parmesan
    cheese, plus extra to serve
salt and ground black pepper
sprigs of flat leaf parsley, to garnish

1 Heat the olive oil in a large frying pan over a medium-high heat. Add the cubes of chicken and cook, stirring occasionally with a wooden spoon, until they start to turn white.

2 Reduce the heat to low and add the chopped onion and garlic. Cook, stirring occasionally, until the onion is soft. Stir in the risotto rice, then sauté for 2 minutes, stirring constantly, until all the rice grains are coated in oil.

3 Add the dry white wine to the rice mixture and cook, stirring constantly, until the wine has been absorbed. Add the saffron threads to the simmering stock and stir well, then add ladlefuls of hot stock to the rice mixture, allowing each ladleful to be fully absorbed before adding the next.

4 When the rice is about three-quarters cooked, add the strips of prosciutto and stir well. Continue cooking, stirring occasionally, until the rice is just tender and the risotto is creamy.

5 Add the butter and the Parmesan and stir in well. Season with salt and pepper to taste. Serve the risotto hot, sprinkled with a little more Parmesan, and garnish with flat leaf parsley.

CASSOULET

Based on the traditional French dish, this recipe is full of delicious flavours and makes a welcoming and warming meal.

SERVES 6

3–4 boneless duck breast portions, about
    450g/1lb total weight
225g/8oz thick-cut streaky (fatty) pork
    or unsmoked streaky (fatty) bacon
    rashers (strips)
450g/1lb Toulouse or garlic sausages
45ml/3 tbsp vegetable oil
450g/1lb onions, chopped
2 garlic cloves, crushed
2 × 425g/15oz cans cannellini beans, rinsed
    and drained
225g/8oz carrots, roughly chopped
400g/14oz can chopped tomatoes
15ml/1 tbsp tomato purée (paste)
bouquet garni
30ml/2 tbsp chopped fresh thyme or
    15ml/1 tbsp dried
475ml/16fl oz/2 cups well-flavoured
    chicken stock
115g/4oz/2 cups fresh white or wholemeal
    (whole-wheat) breadcrumbs
salt and ground black pepper
fresh thyme sprigs, to garnish
warm crusty bread, to serve

1 Preheat the oven to 160°C/325°F/
Gas 3. Cut the duck portions and pork
or bacon rashers into large pieces. Twist
the sausages to shorten them and then
cut them into short lengths.

COOK'S TIP
Cannellini beans are large white beans
with a nutty flavour. They are especially
popular in Italy, particularly in Tuscany,
where they are included in a variety of
pasta and soup dishes. Cannellini beans
are sometimes referred to as white
kidney beans or fazola beans.

2 Heat the oil in a large flameproof
casserole. Cook the meat in batches,
until well browned. Remove from the
pan with a slotted spoon and drain on
kitchen paper.

3 Add the onions and garlic to the pan
and cook for 3–4 minutes, or until
beginning to soften, stirring frequently.

4 Stir in the beans, carrots, tomatoes,
tomato purée, bouquet garni, thyme and
seasoning. Return the meat to the
casserole and mix until well combined.

VARIATION
Canned butter (lima) beans or borlotti
beans can be used in this recipe instead
of the cannellini beans.

5 Add enough of the stock just to cover
the meat and beans. (The cassoulet
shouldn't be swimming in juices; if the
mixture becomes too dry during the
cooking time, add a little more stock or
water.) Bring to the boil. Cover the
casserole tightly and cook in the oven
for 1 hour.

6 Remove the cassoulet from the oven
and add a little more stock or water, if
necessary. Remove the bouquet garni.

7 Sprinkle the breadcrumbs in an even
layer over the top of the cassoulet and
return to the oven, uncovered, for a
further 40 minutes, or until the meat is
tender and the top crisp and lightly
brown. Garnish with fresh thyme sprigs
and serve hot with plenty of warm
crusty bread to mop up the juices.

STIR-FRIED CRISPY DUCK

This stir-fry would be delicious wrapped in flour tortillas or steamed Chinese pancakes, with a little extra warm plum sauce.

2 Heat the oil in a wok or large frying pan and cook the duck over a high heat until golden and crisp. Keep stirring to prevent the duck from sticking. Remove the duck with a slotted spoon and drain on kitchen paper. You may need to cook the duck in several batches.

3 Add the spring onions to the pan and cook for 2 minutes. Stir in the cabbage and cook for 5 minutes, or until it is softened and golden.

SERVES 2

275–350g/10–12oz boneless duck breast
30ml/2 tbsp plain (all-purpose) flour
60ml/4 tbsp oil
1 bunch spring onions (scallions), halved
 lengthwise and cut into 5cm/2in strips,
 plus extra to garnish
275g/10oz/2½ cups finely shredded
 green cabbage
225g/8oz can water chestnuts, drained
 and sliced
50g/2oz/½ cup unsalted cashew nuts
115g/4oz cucumber, cut into strips
45ml/3 tbsp plum sauce
15ml/1 tbsp light soy sauce
salt and ground black pepper

1 Remove any skin from the duck breast, then trim off a little of the fat. Thinly slice the meat into even-size pieces. Season the flour with plenty of salt and pepper and use it to completely coat each piece of duck.

4 Return the duck to the pan with the water chestnuts, cashews and cucumber. Stir-fry for 2 minutes. Add the plum sauce and soy sauce and season to taste, then heat for 2 minutes. Serve garnished with the sliced spring onions.

MEDITERRANEAN DUCK with HARISSA and SAFFRON

Harissa is a fiery chilli sauce from north Africa. Mixed with cinnamon, saffron and preserved lemon, it gives this colourful casserole an unforgettable flavour.

SERVES 4

15ml/1 tbsp olive oil
1.8–2kg/4–4½lb duck, quartered
1 large onion, thinly sliced
1 garlic clove, crushed
2.5ml/½ tsp ground cumin
400ml/14fl oz/1⅔ cups duck or
    chicken stock
juice of ½ lemon
5–10ml/1–2 tsp harissa
1 cinnamon stick
5ml/1 tsp saffron threads
50g/2oz/⅓ cup black olives
50g/2oz/⅓ cup green olives
peel of 1 preserved lemon, rinsed, drained
    and cut into fine strips
2–3 lemon slices
30ml/2 tbsp chopped fresh coriander
    (cilantro), plus extra leaves
    to garnish
salt and ground black pepper

1 Heat the oil in a flameproof casserole. Add the duck quarters and cook until browned all over. Remove the duck with a slotted spoon and set aside. Add the onion and garlic to the oil remaining in the casserole and cook for 5 minutes until soft. Add the ground cumin and cook, stirring, for 2 minutes.

COOK'S TIP

The term "duck" refers to birds over two months old. The rich flavour of duck is best appreciated when a duck reaches its full-grown size. Look for a duck with a supple, waxy skin with a dry appearance. It should have a long body with tender, meaty breasts.

2 Pour in the stock and lemon juice, then add the harissa, cinnamon and saffron. Bring to the boil. Return the duck to the casserole and add the olives, preserved lemon peel and lemon slices. Season with salt and pepper.

3 Lower the heat, partially cover the casserole and simmer gently for about 45 minutes, or until the duck is cooked through. Discard the cinnamon stick. Stir in the chopped coriander and garnish with the coriander leaves.

FISH AND SHELLFISH MAIN MEALS

For a healthy, delicious meal with superb flavour, fish and shellfish are the perfect choice for one-pot cooking. Baked Sea Bream with Tomatoes would make a fine dish for a mid-week family meal, Seafood Risotto is a good choice for an impromptu supper with friends, while a more formal dinner would provide the perfect opportunity for trying something unusual such as Octopus and Red Wine Stew, Fish with Fregola, Moroccan Fish Tagine or a never-fail colourful Seafood Paella.

PENNE with CREAM and SMOKED SALMON

This modern way of serving pasta is popular all over Italy. The three essential ingredients combine together beautifully, and the dish is very quick and easy to make. Accompany with a green salad, ciabatta bread and some sparkling wine for an easy but impressive meal.

SERVES 4

350g/12oz/3 cups dried penne
115g/4oz thinly sliced
    smoked salmon
2–3 fresh thyme sprigs
25g/1oz/2 tbsp unsalted (sweet)
    butter, diced
150ml/¼ pint/⅔ cup extra-thick single
    (light) cream
salt and ground black pepper

VARIATION
Although penne is the traditional pasta to serve with this sauce, it also goes very well with fresh ravioli stuffed with spinach and ricotta.

COOK'S TIP
This dish can be served as an appetizer or a main course.

1 Cook the dried pasta in a large pan of lightly salted boiling water for 10 minutes until it is just tender or according to the instructions on the packet.

2 Meanwhile, using sharp kitchen scissors, cut the smoked salmon slices into thin strips, about 5mm/¼in wide. Strip the leaves from the thyme sprigs and rinse in cold water.

3 Drain the pasta and return it to the pan. Add the butter and heat gently until melted, then stir in the cream with about one-quarter of the smoked salmon and thyme leaves, then season with pepper. Heat gently for 3–4 minutes, stirring all the time. Check the seasoning. Divide among four warmed bowls, top with the remaining salmon and thyme leaves and serve immediately.

TUNA FRITTATA

This is the ultimate meal in a pan — easy to prepare and easy to serve. For a stronger
cheese flavour, try a creamy goat's cheese in place of the soft white cheese.

SERVES 2–3

25g/1oz/2 tbsp butter
15ml/1 tbsp olive oil
1 onion, finely chopped
175g/6oz courgettes (zucchini), halved
    lengthwise and sliced
75g/3oz/1¼ cups brown cap (cremini)
    mushrooms, sliced
50g/2oz asparagus tips
4 eggs, beaten
75g/3oz/⅜ cup soft white (farmer's) cheese
    or ricotta cheese
30ml/2 tbsp chopped fresh thyme
200g/7oz can tuna, in olive oil, drained and
    roughly flaked
115g/4oz cooked, peeled
    prawns (shrimp)
salt and ground black pepper

1 Heat the butter and oil in a non-stick frying pan. Add the chopped onion and cook for 3 minutes, then add the sliced courgettes, mushrooms and asparagus tips and cook for a further 10 minutes, or until beginning to soften and brown.

2 Beat together the eggs, soft or ricotta cheese, chopped thyme and plenty of seasoning until they are well combined.

3 Stir the tuna into the pan, add the prawns and season well. Heat through gently. Pour over the egg mixture and cook over a gentle heat for 5 minutes.

4 Push the egg away from the sides to allow the uncooked egg to run on to the pan. Preheat the grill (broiler) to medium and grill (broil) the omelette to set and brown the surface. Serve cut in wedges.

JANSSON'S TEMPTATION

A traditional Swedish favourite, this rich gratin is utterly moreish. As food writer Jane Grigson pointed out, the name probably does not refer to a specific Jansson but means "everyone's temptation" as Jansson is a common Swedish surname.

SERVES 4–6

50g/2oz/¼ cup butter
900g/2lb potatoes
2 large, sweet onions, sliced
2 × 50g/2oz cans anchovies in olive
    oil, drained
450ml/¾ pint/scant 2 cups whipping cream
    or half and half double (heavy) and
    single (light) cream
a little milk (optional)
salt and ground black pepper

1 Preheat the oven to 200°C/400°F/ Gas 6. Use 15g/½oz/1 tbsp of the butter to grease a shallow 1.5 litre/2½ pint/ 6¼ cup earthenware baking dish.

2 Using a small sharp knife, carefully cut the potatoes into thin slices, then cut the slices into fine matchstick strips.

3 Toss the potato strips with salt and ground black pepper and sprinkle half of them in the base of the prepared ovenproof dish.

COOK'S TIPS
• It is important to cover the gratin with foil for the first half of the cooking time so that the potatoes don't brown or dry out too much.
• If using whole, salted anchovies or Swedish salted sprats (US small whitebait or smelts) they will need to be boned. If they are very salty, soak in a little milk for about 30 minutes before using.
• Serve with small glasses of chilled schnapps and cold beer for an authentic Swedish flavour.

4 Lay half of the onions on top of the potatoes, season with black pepper and dot with butter. Lay the anchovies on top of the onions, then add the rest of the sliced onions and top with the remaining potatoes.

5 Mix the cream with 30ml/2 tbsp cold water and pour this mixture over the potatoes and onions in the dish. Add a little milk, if necessary, to bring the liquid to just below the top of the final layer of potato matchstick strips.

6 Dot the potatoes with the remaining butter, then cover the dish with foil and bake for 1 hour.

7 Reduce the oven temperature to 180°C/350°F/Gas 4 and remove the foil from the top of the dish. Bake for a further 40–50 minutes, or until the potatoes are tender when tested with a knife and brown in colour.

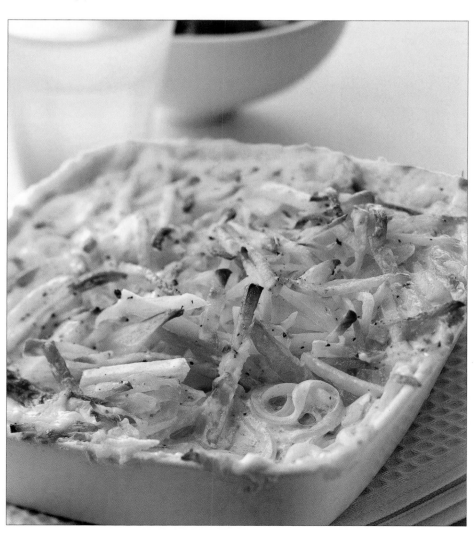

FILLETS of BRILL in RED WINE SAUCE

Forget the old maxim that red wine and fish do not go well together. The robust sauce adds colour and richness to this excellent dish, which is more than elegant enough for a dinner party. Halibut and John Dory are also good cooked this way.

SERVES 4

4 fillets of brill, about 175–200g/6–7oz
    each, skinned
150g/5oz/10 tbsp chilled butter, diced, plus
    extra for greasing
115g/4oz shallots, thinly sliced
200ml/7fl oz/scant 1 cup robust red wine
200ml/7fl oz/scant 1 cup fish stock
salt and ground black and white pepper
fresh flat leaf parsley leaves or chervil,
    to garnish

1 Preheat the oven to 180°C/350°F/ Gas 4. Season the fish fillets on both sides with salt and ground black pepper. Generously butter a shallow flameproof dish, which is large enough to take all the brill fillets in a single layer. Spread the shallots in an even layer in the dish and lay the fish fillets on top. Season well with salt and ground black pepper.

2 Pour in the red wine and fish stock, cover the dish with a lid or foil and then bring the liquid to just below boiling point. Transfer the dish to the oven and bake for 6–8 minutes, or until the brill is just cooked.

3 Using a fish slice (metal spatula), lift the fish and shallots on to a serving dish, cover with foil and keep hot.

4 Transfer the dish to the stove and bring the cooking liquid to the boil over a high heat. Cook it until it has reduced by half. Lower the heat and whisk in the chilled butter, one piece at a time, to make a smooth, shiny sauce. Season with salt and ground white pepper, set the sauce aside and keep hot.

5 Divide the shallots among four warmed plates and lay the brill fillets on top. Pour the sauce over and around the fish and garnish with the fresh flat leaf parsley or chervil.

BAKED MONKFISH with POTATOES and GARLIC

This simple supper dish can be made with other fish. Sauce tartare or a thick vinaigrette
flavoured with chopped gherkins and hard-boiled egg are delicious accompaniments.

3 Pour the main batch of stock over the potatoes and bake, uncovered, stirring once or twice, for about 50 minutes, or until the potatoes are just tender.

4 Nestle the monkfish tail into the potatoes and season well with salt and ground black pepper. Mix the 45ml/ 3 tbsp stock with the wine and use to baste the monkfish two or three times during cooking. Bake the monkfish and potatoes for 10–15 minutes.

SERVES 4

50g/2oz/¼ cup butter
2 onions, thickly sliced
1kg/2¼lb waxy potatoes, peeled and cut
    into small chunks
4 garlic cloves
a few fresh thyme sprigs
2–3 fresh bay leaves
450ml/¾ pint/scant 2 cups vegetable
    or fish stock, plus 45ml/3 tbsp
900g/2lb monkfish tail in one piece,
    membrane removed
30–45ml/2–3 tbsp white wine
50g/2oz/1 cup fresh white breadcrumbs
15g/½oz fresh flat leaf parsley,
    finely chopped
15ml/1 tbsp olive oil
salt and ground black pepper

1 Preheat the oven to 190°C/375°F/ Gas 5. Melt half the butter in a shallow flameproof dish and cook the onions for 5 minutes until soft. Stir in the potatoes.

2 Slice two of the garlic cloves and add them to the dish with the thyme and bay leaves, and season with salt and pepper.

5 Finely chop the remaining garlic. Melt the remaining butter and toss it with the fresh breadcrumbs, chopped garlic, most of the chopped parsley and seasoning. Spread the crumb mixture over the monkfish, pressing it down gently with the back of a spoon.

6 Drizzle the olive oil over the crumb-covered fish, then return the dish to the oven and bake for a final 10–15 minutes, or until the breadcrumbs are crisp and golden brown and all the liquid has been absorbed. Sprinkle the remaining chopped parsley on to the potatoes and fish and serve immediately.

FISH with SPINACH and LIME

Fresh herbs and hot spices are combined to make the charmoula marinade that is used to
flavour this delicious Moroccan-style dish. Crusty bread makes a good accompaniment.

SERVES 4

675g/1½lb white fish, such as haddock,
    cod, sea bass or monkfish
sunflower oil, for frying
500g/1¼lb potatoes, sliced
1 onion, chopped
1–2 garlic cloves, crushed
5 tomatoes, peeled and chopped
375g/13oz fresh spinach, chopped
lime wedges, to garnish

For the charmoula
6 spring onions (scallions), chopped
10ml/2 tsp fresh thyme
60ml/4 tbsp chopped flat leaf parsley
30ml/2 tbsp chopped fresh
    coriander (cilantro)
10ml/2 tsp paprika
generous pinch of cayenne pepper
60ml/4 tbsp olive oil
grated rind of 1 lime and 60ml/4 tbsp
    lime juice
salt

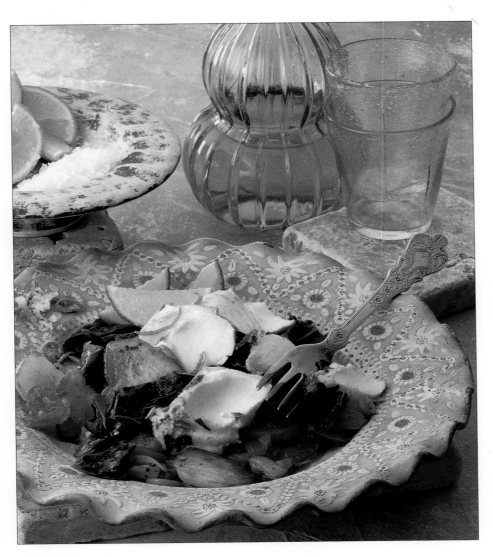

1 Cut the white fish into large even-size pieces, discarding any skin and bones. Place the fish in a large shallow dish.

2 Blend together the ingredients for the charmoula. Season with salt. Pour over the fish, stir to mix and leave in a cool place, covered with clear film (plastic wrap), to marinate for 2–4 hours.

3 Heat about 5mm/¼in oil in a large heavy pan, add the potato slices and cook, turning them occasionally, until they are cooked right through and golden brown. Drain the fried potatoes on kitchen paper.

4 Pour off all but 15ml/1 tbsp of the oil from the pan and add the onion, garlic and tomatoes. Cook over a gentle heat for 5–6 minutes, stirring occasionally, until the onion is soft. Place the potatoes on top and then add the spinach.

5 Place the marinated fish pieces on top of the chopped spinach in the pan and pour over all of the marinade. Cover the pan tightly and cook for 15–18 minutes. After about 8 minutes of the cooking time, carefully stir the contents of the pan with a wooden spoon, so that the pieces of fish at the top are distributed throughout the dish.

6 Cover the pan again and continue cooking, but check occasionally – the dish is cooked once the fish is just tender and opaque and the spinach has wilted. Serve the dish hot, with wedges of lime and plenty of warm crusty bread, if you like.

BAKED SEA BREAM with TOMATOES

John Dory, halibut or sea bass can all be cooked this way. If you prefer to use filleted fish, choose a chunky fillet, such as cod, and roast it skin-side up. Roasting the tomatoes brings out their sweetness, which contrasts beautifully with the flavour of the fish.

SERVES 4–6

8 ripe tomatoes
10ml/2 tsp sugar
200ml/7fl oz/scant 1 cup olive oil
450g/1lb new potatoes
1 lemon, sliced
1 bay leaf
1 fresh thyme sprig
8 fresh basil leaves
1 sea bream, about 900g–1kg/2–2¼lb,
    cleaned and scaled
150ml/¼ pint/⅔ cup dry white wine
30ml/2 tbsp fresh white breadcrumbs
2 garlic cloves, crushed
15ml/1 tbsp finely chopped fresh parsley
salt and ground black pepper
fresh flat parsley or basil leaves, chopped,
    to garnish

1 Preheat the oven to 240°C/475°F/ Gas 9. Cut the tomatoes in half lengthwise and arrange them in a single layer in a baking dish, cut-side up. Sprinkle with sugar, salt and pepper and drizzle over a little of the olive oil. Roast for 30–40 minutes, until lightly browned. Remove the tomatoes from the dish and set aside.

2 Meanwhile, cut the potatoes into 1cm/½in slices. Place in a large pan of salted water and par-boil for 5 minutes. Drain and set aside.

3 Grease the baking dish with a little more of the oil. Arrange the potatoes in a single layer with the lemon slices over; sprinkle on the herbs. Season and drizzle with half the remaining oil. Lay the fish on top and season. Pour over the wine and the rest of the oil. Arrange the tomatoes around the fish.

4 Mix together the breadcrumbs, garlic and parsley; sprinkle over the fish. Bake for 30 minutes. Garnish with chopped parsley or basil.

FISH with FREGOLA

This Sardinian speciality is a cross between a soup and a stew. Serve it with crusty Italian country bread to mop up the juices.

SERVES 4–6

75ml/5 tbsp olive oil
4 garlic cloves, finely chopped
½ small fresh red chilli, seeded and
    finely chopped
I large handful fresh flat leaf parsley,
    roughly chopped
I red snapper, about 450g/1lb, cleaned,
    with head and tail removed
I grey mullet or porgy, about 500g/1¼lb,
    cleaned, with head and tail removed
350–450g/12oz–1lb thick cod fillet
400g/14oz can chopped plum tomatoes
175g/6oz/1½ cups dried fregola
250ml/8fl oz/1 cup water
salt and ground black pepper

1 Heat 30ml/2 tbsp of the olive oil in a large flameproof casserole. Add the chopped garlic and chilli, with about half the chopped fresh parsley. Fry over a medium heat, stirring occasionally, for about 5 minutes.

2 Cut all of the fish into large chunks – including the skin and the bones in the case of the snapper and mullet – and add the pieces to the casserole. Sprinkle with a further 30ml/2 tbsp of the olive oil and fry for a few minutes more.

3 Add the tomatoes, then fill the empty can with water and add to the pan. Bring to the boil. Season to taste, lower the heat and cook for 10 minutes.

4 Add the fregola and simmer for about 5 minutes, then add the water and the remaining oil. Simmer for 15 minutes until the fregola is just tender.

5 If the sauce becomes too thick, add more water, then taste for seasoning. Serve hot, in warmed bowls, sprinkled with the remaining parsley.

VARIATION
Any white fish fillet can be used instead of cod in this dish. Monkfish, haddock, hake or plaice could all be used.

COOK'S TIPS
• Fregola is a tiny pasta shape from Sardinia. If you can't get it, use a tiny soup pasta (*pastina*), such as *corallini* or *semi de melone*.
• You can make the basic fish sauce several hours in advance or even the day before, bringing it to the boil and adding the fregola just before serving.

FISH PLAKI

Greece has so much coastline, it's no wonder that fish is so popular there. Generally, it is treated simply, but in this recipe the fish is cooked with onions and tomatoes.

SERVES 6

300ml/½ pint/1¼ cups olive oil
2 onions, thinly sliced
3 large, well-flavoured tomatoes, roughly chopped
3 garlic cloves, thinly sliced
5ml/1 tsp sugar
5ml/1 tsp chopped fresh dill
5ml/1 tsp chopped fresh mint
5ml/1 tsp chopped fresh celery leaves
15ml/1 tbsp chopped fresh flat leaf parsley
300ml/½ pint/1¼ cups water
6 hake or cod steaks
juice of 1 lemon
salt and ground black pepper
extra fresh dill, mint or parsley sprigs, to garnish

1 Heat the oil in large heavy sauté pan or flameproof casserole. Add the onions and cook, stirring, until pale golden, then add the tomatoes, garlic, sugar, dill, mint, celery leaves and parsley with the water. Season with salt and pepper, then simmer, uncovered, for 25 minutes, until the liquid has reduced by one-third.

2 Add the fish steaks and cook gently for 10–12 minutes until the fish is just cooked. Remove the pan or casserole from the heat and add the lemon juice. Cover and leave to stand for 20 minutes before serving. Arrange the cod in a dish and pour the sauce over. Garnish with herbs and serve warm or cold.

MOROCCAN FISH TAGINE

This spicy, aromatic dish proves just how exciting an ingredient fish can be. Serve it with couscous, which you can steam in the traditional way in a colander on top of the tagine.

SERVES 8

1.3kg/3lb firm fish fillets, skinned and cut
    into 5cm/2in chunks
60ml/4 tbsp olive oil
1 large aubergine (eggplant), cut into
    1cm/½in cubes
2 courgettes (zucchini), cut into
    1cm/½in cubes
4 onions, chopped
400g/14oz can chopped tomatoes
400ml/14fl oz/1⅔ cups passata (bottled
    strained tomatoes)
200ml/7fl oz/scant 1 cup fish stock
1 preserved lemon, chopped
90g/3½oz/scant 1 cup olives
60ml/4 tbsp chopped fresh coriander
    (cilantro), plus extra coriander leaves
    to garnish
salt and ground black pepper

For the harissa
3 large fresh red chillies, seeded
    and chopped
3 garlic cloves, peeled
15ml/1 tbsp ground coriander
30ml/2 tbsp ground cumin
5ml/1 tsp ground cinnamon
grated rind of 1 lemon
30ml/2 tbsp sunflower oil

1 Make the harissa. Whizz everything in a food processor to a smooth paste.

2 Put the fish in a wide bowl and add 30ml/2 tbsp of the harissa. Toss to coat, cover and chill for at least 1 hour.

COOK'S TIP
To make the fish go further, add 225g/8oz/
1¼ cups cooked chickpeas to the tagine.

3 Heat half the olive oil in a shallow heavy pan. Add the aubergine cubes and fry for about 10 minutes, or until they are golden brown. Add the courgettes and fry for a further 2 minutes. Remove the vegetables from the pan using a slotted spoon and set aside.

4 Add the remaining olive oil to the pan, add the onions and cook over a low heat for about 10 minutes until golden brown. Stir in the remaining harissa and cook for 5 minutes, stirring occasionally.

5 Add the vegetables and combine with the onions, then stir in the chopped tomatoes, the passata and fish stock. Bring to the boil, then lower the heat and simmer for about 20 minutes.

6 Stir the fish chunks and preserved lemon into the pan. Add the olives and stir gently. Cover and simmer over a low heat for about 15–20 minutes. Season to taste. Stir in the chopped coriander. Serve with couscous, if you like, and garnish with coriander leaves.

ITALIAN FISH STEW

Italians are renowned for enjoying good food, and this stew is a veritable feast of fish and shellfish in a delicious tomato broth — ideal for a family lunch.

SERVES 4

30ml/2 tbsp olive oil
1 onion, thinly sliced
a few saffron threads
5ml/1 tsp dried thyme
large pinch of cayenne pepper
2 garlic cloves, finely chopped
2 × 400g/14oz cans tomatoes, drained
   and chopped
175ml/6fl oz/¾ cup dry white wine
2 litres/3½ pints/8 cups hot fish stock
350g/12oz white, skinless fish fillets, such
   as haddock or cod, cut into pieces
450g/1lb monkfish, cut into pieces
450g/1lb mussels, scrubbed
225g/8oz small squid, cleaned and cut
   into rings
30ml/2 tbsp chopped fresh basil
   or parsley
salt and ground black pepper
thickly sliced bread, to serve

1 Heat the olive oil in a large, heavy pan. Add the onion, saffron threads, thyme, cayenne pepper and salt, to taste. Stir well and cook over a low heat for 10 minutes, until the onion is soft. Add the garlic and cook for 1 minute more.

2 Stir in the chopped tomatoes, dry white wine and hot fish stock. Bring to the boil and boil for 1 minute, then reduce the heat and simmer gently for 15 minutes.

COOK'S TIP
Cayenne pepper has quite a hot, spicy flavour and was originally made from a type of chilli from the Cayenne region of French Guiana. It should be used sparingly.

3 Add the fish pieces to the tomato mixture in the pan and stir gently. Simmer the stew over a low heat for a further 3 minutes.

4 Add the mussels and squid rings and simmer for about 2 minutes, until the mussels open. Discard any that remain closed. Stir in the basil or parsley and season to taste. Ladle into warmed soup bowls and serve with bread.

FISH STEW with LEMON GRASS

*Lemon grass and ginger give this delicate stew of fish, prawns, new potatoes and broccoli
an appetizing aromatic flavour.*

SERVES 4

25g/1oz/2 tbsp butter
175g/6oz onions, chopped
20ml/4 tsp plain (all-purpose) flour
400ml/14fl oz/1⅔ cups light fish stock
150ml/¼ pint/⅔ cup white wine
2.5cm/1in piece fresh root ginger, peeled
    and finely chopped
2 lemon grass stalks, trimmed and
    finely chopped
450g/1lb new potatoes, scrubbed and
    halved if necessary
450g/1lb white fish fillets
175g/6oz large, cooked, peeled
    prawns (shrimp)
275g/10oz small broccoli florets
150ml/¼ pint/⅔ cup double (heavy) cream
60ml/4 tbsp chopped fresh garlic chives
salt and ground black pepper
crusty bread, to serve

3 Remove the skin from the fish fillets
and cut the fillets into large chunks. Add
the chunks of fish to the pan with the
prawns, broccoli and cream. Stir gently.

4 Simmer gently for 5 minutes, taking
care not to break up the fish. Adjust
the seasoning and sprinkle in the chives.
Serve with plenty of crusty bread.

1 Melt the butter in a large pan. Add
the onions and cook for 3–4 minutes.
Stir in the flour and cook for 1 minute.

2 Stir in the stock, wine, ginger, lemon
grass and potatoes. Season and bring to
the boil. Cover and cook for 15 minutes,
or until the potatoes are almost tender.

COD and PRAWN GREEN COCONUT CURRY

This quick curry takes just minutes to make. If you can't find green masala curry paste at your local supermarket, simply substitute another variety – the curry will be just as good.

SERVES 4

675g/1½lb cod fillets, skinned
90ml/6 tbsp green masala curry paste
175ml/6fl oz/¾ cup canned coconut
    milk or 200ml/7fl oz/scant 1 cup
    coconut cream
175g/6oz raw or cooked, peeled
    prawns (shrimp)
fresh coriander (cilantro), to garnish
basmati rice, to serve

VARIATION
Any firm fish, such as monkfish, can be used instead of cod. Whole fish steaks can be cooked in the sauce, but allow an extra 5 minutes' cooking time and baste them with the sauce from time to time.

1 Using a sharp knife, cut the skinned cod fillets into 4cm/1½in pieces.

2 Put the green masala curry paste and the coconut milk or cream into a frying pan. Heat to simmering and simmer gently for 5 minutes, stirring occasionally.

3 Add the cod pieces and prawns (if raw) to the cream mixture and cook gently for 5 minutes. If using cooked prawns, then add them after this time and heat through. Garnish the curry with fresh coriander and serve immediately with basmati rice.

OCTOPUS and RED WINE STEW

Fresh octopus can be quite tricky to prepare so unless you're happy to clean and prepare it for this traditional Greek dish, buy one that's ready for cooking.

SERVES 4

900g/2lb prepared octopus
450g/1lb onions, sliced
2 bay leaves
450g/1lb ripe tomatoes
60ml/4 tbsp olive oil
4 garlic cloves, crushed
5ml/1 tsp sugar
15ml/1 tbsp chopped fresh oregano
　　or rosemary
30ml/2 tbsp chopped fresh parsley
150ml/¼ pint/⅔ cup red wine
30ml/2 tbsp red wine vinegar
chopped fresh herbs, to garnish
warm bread and pine nuts, to serve

COOK'S TIP
The octopus, along with cuttlefish and squid, is a member of the mollusc family – their main shared characteristic is that they have no shell. Octopus can be very tough, so it needs long, slow cooking to tenderize it.

1 Put the octopus in a large pan of gently simmering water with one-quarter of the onions and the bay leaves. Cover the pan and cook gently for 1 hour.

2 While the octopus is cooking, plunge the tomatoes into boiling water for 30 seconds, then refresh in cold water. Peel away the skins and chop roughly.

3 Drain the octopus and, using a small sharp knife, cut it into bitesize pieces. Discard the head.

4 Heat the oil in the pan and fry the octopus, the remaining onions and the garlic for 3 minutes. Add the tomatoes, sugar, herbs, wine and vinegar and cook, stirring, for 5 minutes.

5 Cover the pan and cook over the lowest possible heat for about 1½ hours until the red wine and tomato sauce is thickened and the octopus is tender. To serve, garnish with fresh herbs and serve with plenty of warm bread, and pine nuts to scatter on top.

MUSSELS and CLAMS with LEMON GRASS and COCONUT CREAM

Lemon grass has an incomparable flavour and aroma and is widely used in Thai cooking, especially with seafood. If you have difficulty obtaining fresh baby clams for this recipe, then use a few extra mussels instead.

SERVES 6

1.8–2kg/4–4½lb mussels
450g/1lb baby clams
120ml/4fl oz/½ cup dry white wine
1 bunch spring onions (scallions), chopped
2 lemon grass stalks, chopped
6 kaffir lime leaves, chopped
10ml/2 tsp Thai green curry paste
200ml/7fl oz/scant 1 cup coconut cream
30ml/2 tbsp chopped fresh
    coriander (cilantro)
salt and ground black pepper
garlic chives, to garnish

1 Clean the mussels by pulling off the beards, scrubbing the shells well and removing any barnacles. Discard any broken mussels or any that do not close when tapped sharply. Wash the clams.

COOK'S TIP
The kaffir lime tree is native to South-east Asia and both the leaves and fruit rind are used in cooking. Dried kaffir lime leaves, available from supermarkets, can be used in place of fresh – add them at the beginning of the cooking time and remove and discard just before serving.

2 Put the white wine in a large, heavy pan with the spring onions, chopped lemon grass stalks, kaffir lime leaves and Thai green curry paste. Simmer all the ingredients together until the wine has almost evaporated.

3 Add the mussels and clams to the pan, cover tightly and steam the shellfish over a high heat for 5–6 minutes, or until they open.

4 Using a slotted spoon, transfer the cooked mussels and clams to a heated serving bowl and keep hot. At this stage discard any shellfish that remain closed. Strain the cooking liquid into the clean pan and gently simmer until it is reduced to about 250ml/8fl oz/1 cup.

5 Stir in the coconut cream and fresh coriander, with plenty of salt and pepper to taste. Increase the heat and simmer gently until the sauce is piping hot. Pour the sauce over the mussels and clams and serve immediately, garnished with garlic chives.

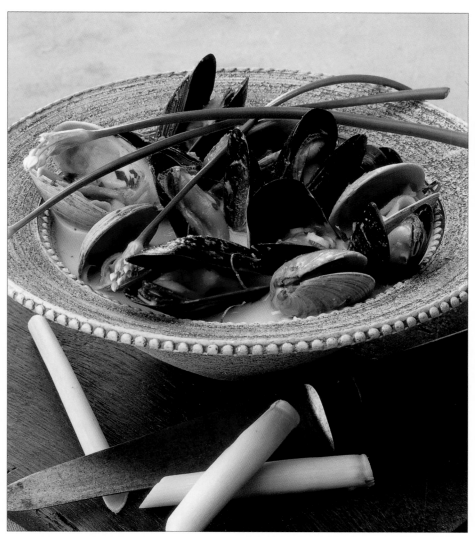

GINGERED SEAFOOD STIR-FRY

This would make a lovely summer supper. Serve with lots of bread to mop up the juices
and some chilled dry white wine. It would also be good as a first course for four.

SERVES 2

15ml/1 tbsp sunflower oil
5ml/1 tsp sesame oil
2.5cm/1in piece fresh root ginger, peeled
    and finely chopped
1 bunch spring onions (scallions), sliced
1 red (bell) pepper, seeded and
    finely chopped
115g/4oz small "queen" scallops
8 large, raw prawns (shrimp), peeled
115g/4oz squid rings
15ml/1 tbsp lime juice
15ml/1 tbsp light soy sauce
60ml/4 tbsp coconut milk
salt and ground black pepper
mixed salad leaves and crusty bread,
    to serve

1 Heat the sunflower and sesame oils in a wok or large frying pan and cook the chopped ginger and sliced spring onions for 2–3 minutes, stirring frequently, until golden brown. Add the chopped red pepper and cook, stirring constantly, for a further 3 minutes.

2 Add the scallops, prawns and squid rings to the wok or frying pan and cook over a medium heat for about 3 minutes stirring occasionally with a wooden spoon, until all the seafood is opaque and just cooked through. Add the lime juice and light soy sauce.

3 Pour in the coconut milk and mix well, then simmer the sauce, uncovered, for 2 minutes, until the sauce begins to thicken slightly.

4 Season the stir-fry well. Arrange the mixed salad leaves on two individual serving plates and spoon over the seafood mixture with the juices. Serve the seafood with plenty of crusty bread to mop up the juices.

SEAFOOD PAELLA

There are as many versions of paella as there are regions of Spain. Those from near the coast contain a lot of seafood, while inland versions add chicken or pork. Here the only meat is the chorizo – essential for an authentic flavour.

SERVES 4

45ml/3 tbsp olive oil
1 large onion, chopped
2 fat garlic cloves, chopped
150g/5oz chorizo, sliced
300g/11oz small squid, cleaned
1 red (bell) pepper, seeded and sliced
4 tomatoes, peeled, seeded and diced,
    or 200g/7oz can tomatoes
about 500ml/17fl oz/generous 2 cups
    chicken stock
105ml/7 tbsp dry white wine
200g/7oz/1 cup short grain Spanish rice
    or risotto rice
a large pinch of saffron threads
150g/5oz/1¼ cups fresh or frozen peas
12 large cooked prawns (shrimp), in the
    shell, or 8 langoustines
450g/1lb mussels, scrubbed
450g/1lb clams, scrubbed
salt and ground black pepper

1 Heat the olive oil in a large sauté pan or a paella pan, add the onion and garlic and fry until the onion is translucent. Add the chorizo and fry until golden.

2 If the squid are very small, you can leave them whole; otherwise cut the bodies into rings and the tentacles into pieces. Add the squid to the pan and sauté over a high heat for 2 minutes, stirring occasionally.

3 Stir in the pepper slices and the seeded and diced tomatoes and simmer gently for 5 minutes, until the pepper slices are tender. Pour in the stock and wine, stir well and bring to the boil.

4 Stir in the rice and saffron and season to taste with salt and pepper. Spread the contents of the pan in an even layer over the base. Bring the liquid back to the boil, then lower the heat and simmer gently for 10 minutes.

5 Add the peas, prawns or langoustines, mussels and clams, stirring them gently into the rice. Cook gently for another 15–20 minutes, until the rice is tender and all the mussels and clams have opened. If any remain closed, discard them. If the paella seems dry, add a little more stock. Gently stir everything together and serve piping hot.

SEAFOOD RISOTTO

Creamy, saffron-flavoured rice makes the perfect foil for shellfish. Ready-prepared, frozen seafood mixtures, which include prawns, squid and mussels, are ideal for making this quick and easy dish – remember to thaw them before cooking.

SERVES 4

1 litre/1¾ pints/4 cups hot fish or
   shellfish stock
50g/2oz/¼ cup unsalted (sweet) butter
2 shallots, chopped
2 garlic cloves, chopped
350g/12oz/1¾ cups risotto rice
150ml/¼ pint/⅔ cup dry white wine
2.5ml/½ tsp powdered saffron, or a
   pinch of saffron threads
400g/14oz mixed prepared seafood,
   thawed if frozen
30ml/2 tbsp freshly grated
   Parmesan cheese
30ml/2 tbsp chopped fresh flat leaf parsley,
   to garnish
salt and ground black pepper

1 Pour the fish or shellfish stock into a large, heavy pan. Bring it to the boil, then pour it into a large, heatproof jug (pitcher) or bowl and keep warm.

2 Melt the butter in the rinsed-out pan pan, add the shallots and garlic and cook over a low heat for 3–5 minutes, stirring occasionally, until the shallots are soft but not coloured. Add the rice, stir well to coat the grains completely with butter, then pour in the dry white wine. Cook over a medium heat, stirring occasionally, until the wine has been absorbed by the rice.

COOK'S TIP
It is essential to use proper risotto rice, such as arborio or carnaroli, for this dish. It has a wonderfully creamy texture when cooked but still retains a "bite".

3 Add a ladleful of hot stock and the saffron, and cook, stirring continuously, until the liquid has been absorbed. Add the seafood and stir well. Continue to add hot stock a ladleful at a time, waiting until each quantity has been absorbed before adding more. Stir the mixture for about 20 minutes in all until the rice is swollen and creamy, but still with a little bite in the middle.

VARIATION
Use peeled prawns (shrimp), or cubes of fish such as cod or salmon in place of the mixed prepared seafood.

4 Vigorously mix in the freshly grated Parmesan cheese and season to taste, then sprinkle over the chopped parsley and serve immediately.

VEGETARIAN MAIN MEALS AND PASTA

The great thing about these vegetarian dishes is that many of them are made with ingredients you will almost certainly have in your kitchen, so they are the recipes you'll make time and time again for all the family. Pan Haggerty, for instance, owes its excellent flavour to three simple ingredients: potatoes, Cheddar cheese and chives. Vegetable Korma is very adaptable, and Fettucine with Butter and Parmesan is as easy as its name suggests.

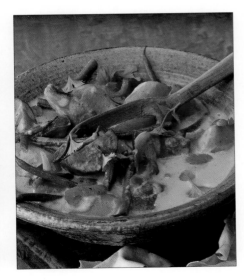

NEW POTATOES and VEGETABLES BAKED TURKISH-STYLE

Here's a meal in a pot that's suitable for feeding large numbers of people. It's lightly spiced and has plenty of garlic – who could refuse?

SERVES 4

60ml/4 tbsp olive oil
1 large onion, chopped
2 aubergines (eggplant), cut into
    small cubes
4 courgettes (zucchini), cut into
    small chunks
1 green (bell) pepper, seeded
    and chopped
1 red or yellow (bell) pepper,
    seeded and chopped
115g/4oz/1 cup fresh or frozen peas
115g/4oz green beans
450g/1lb new or salad potatoes, cubed
2.5ml/½ tsp ground cinnamon
2.5ml/½ tsp ground cumin
5ml/1 tsp paprika
4–5 tomatoes, skinned
400g/14oz can chopped tomatoes
30ml/2 tbsp chopped fresh parsley
3–4 garlic cloves, crushed
350ml/12fl oz/1½ cups vegetable stock
salt and ground black pepper
black olives and fresh parsley,
    to garnish

1 Preheat the oven to 190°C/375°F/ Gas 5. Heat 45ml/3 tbsp of the oil in a large frying pan, add the onion and fry until golden.

2 Add the aubergine and sauté for about 3 minutes, then add the courgette, chopped peppers, peas, beans and cubed potatoes, together with the cinnamon, cumin, paprika and seasoning. Continue to cook for a further 3 minutes, stirring the mixture constantly. Transfer the vegetables to an ovenproof dish.

3 Halve the fresh tomatoes, remove the seeds using a teaspoon and then chop the tomato flesh. Mix the tomato flesh with the canned tomatoes, chopped parsley, crushed garlic and the remaining olive oil in a bowl.

4 Pour the vegetable stock over the aubergine and pepper mixture and then spoon the prepared tomato mixture evenly over the top. Cover the dish with foil and bake for 30–45 minutes. Serve hot, garnished with olives and parsley.

MEDITERRANEAN VEGETABLES BAKED in GOLDEN BATTER

Crunchy golden batter surrounds these vegetables, making them delicious and filling. Serve with salad as a light lunch, or with grilled sausages for a more substantial meal.

SERVES 6

1 small aubergine (eggplant), trimmed,
  halved and thickly sliced
1 egg
115g/4oz/1 cup plain (all-purpose) flour
300ml/½ pint/1¼ cups milk
30ml/2 tbsp fresh thyme leaves, or
  10ml/2 tsp dried
1 red onion
2 large courgettes (zucchini)
1 red (bell) pepper
1 yellow (bell) pepper
60–75ml/4–5 tbsp sunflower oil
30ml/2 tbsp freshly grated
  Parmesan cheese
salt and ground black pepper
fresh herbs, to garnish

1 Place the aubergine in a colander or sieve, sprinkle generously with salt and leave for 10 minutes. Drain, rinse well and pat dry on kitchen paper.

2 Meanwhile, beat the egg in a bowl, then gradually beat in the flour and a little milk to make a smooth thick paste. Gradually blend in the rest of the milk, add the thyme leaves and seasoning to taste and stir until smooth. Leave the batter in a cool place until required. Preheat the oven to 220°C/425°F/Gas 7.

COOK'S TIP

As with Yorkshire pudding, it is essential to get the fat in the dish really hot before adding the batter, which should sizzle slightly as it goes in. If the fat is not hot enough, the batter will not rise well. Use a dish that is not too deep.

3 Cut the onion into quarters, slice the courgettes and seed and quarter the peppers. Put the oil in a shallow baking tray or roasting pan and heat in the oven. Add the prepared vegetables, toss them in the oil to coat thoroughly and return the pan to the oven for 20 minutes.

4 Give the batter another whisk, then pour it over the vegetables and return to the oven for about 30 minutes. When the batter is puffed up and golden, reduce the heat to 190°C/375°F/Gas 5 for about 10 minutes, or until the edges are crisp. Sprinkle with Parmesan and herbs.

TRUFFADE

Baked until meltingly soft, this warming cheese and potato supper is the perfect slow bake to come home to. In France, where it originated, it would be made with a Tomme or Cantal cheese – look for them in good cheese stores.

SERVES 4–6

a little sunflower oil or melted butter
1 large onion, thinly sliced
675g/1½lb baking potatoes, very
    thinly sliced
150g/5oz/1¼ cups grated hard cheese,
    such as Tomme, Cantal or mature
    (sharp) Cheddar
freshly grated nutmeg
salt and ground black pepper
mixed salad leaves, to serve

VARIATION
In France, they make a non-vegetarian version of this dish, which is cooked with finely diced fatty bacon (lardons) and the cheese is chopped, not grated. The ingredients are mixed and cooked slowly in a little lard in a heavy frying pan on top of the stove.

1 Preheat the oven to 180°C/350°F/ Gas 4. Lightly grease the base of a shallow baking dish or roasting pan with the oil or melted butter.

2 Arrange a layer of sliced onion over the base of the dish, then add a layer of sliced potatoes and about half of the grated cheese. Finish with the remaining onions and a layer of sliced potatoes.

3 Brush the top layer of potatoes with oil or melted butter and season with nutmeg, salt and pepper.

4 Sprinkle the remaining grated cheese over the top and bake for about 1 hour, or until the vegetables are tender and the top is golden brown. Leave the dish to stand for about 5 minutes, then serve cut in wedges with a salad.

POTATOES BAKED with TOMATOES

This simple, hearty dish from the south of Italy is best made in the summer when fresh, ripe tomatoes are in season and bursting with flavour.

SERVES 6

90ml/6 tbsp olive oil
2 large red or yellow onions, thinly sliced
1kg/2¼lb baking potatoes, thinly sliced
450g/1lb well-flavoured tomatoes, sliced,
    with their juice
115g/4oz/1 cup freshly grated Parmesan or
    Cheddar cheese
a few fresh basil leaves
50ml/2fl oz/¼ cup water
salt and ground black pepper

1 Preheat the oven to 180°C/350°F/ Gas 4. Brush a large baking dish generously with 30ml/2 tbsp of the oil.

2 Arrange a layer of some of the thinly sliced onions in the base of the prepared dish, followed by a layer of the potatoes and tomatoes.

3 Drizzle a little of the olive oil over the potatoes and tomatoes, and sprinkle with some of the grated cheese. Season generously with plenty of salt and ground black pepper.

4 Continue to layer the vegetables in the dish until they are used up, ending with an overlapping layer of potatoes and tomatoes.

5 Reserve a sprig of fresh basil for the garnish, tear the remaining leaves into small pieces, and add them here and there among the vegetables. Sprinkle the top with the remaining grated cheese and drizzle with the rest of the oil. Pour the water evenly over the vegetables and cheese, then bake for about 1 hour, or until the vegetables are tender.

6 Check towards the end of the cooking time and, if the top begins to brown too much, place a sheet of foil, baking parchment or a flat baking tray on top of the dish. Garnish with the remaining basil, once it is cooked, and serve hot.

VARIATION
If you can't get hold of really flavoursome tomatoes, a 400g/14oz can of chopped plum tomatoes can be used instead.

FRITTATA with LEEK, RED PEPPER and SPINACH

Apart from the fact that Italian frittata does not usually contain potato and is generally slightly softer in texture, it is not hugely different from Spanish tortilla. This combination of sweet leek, red pepper and spinach is delicious with the egg.

3 Add the spinach and cover the pan. Allow the spinach to wilt in the steam for 3–4 minutes, then stir to mix it into the vegetables, adding the pine nuts.

4 Beat the eggs with salt, pepper, the remaining cumin, basil and parsley. Add to the pan and cook over a gentle heat until the base of the omelette sets and turns golden brown. Pull the edges of the omelette away from the sides of the pan as it cooks and tilt the pan so that the uncooked egg runs underneath.

5 Preheat the grill (broiler). Flash the frittata under the hot grill to set the egg on top, but do not let it become too brown. Cut the frittata into wedges and serve warm, garnished with watercress and sprinkled with Parmesan, if using.

VARIATION

A delicious way to serve frittata is to pack it into a slightly hollowed-out loaf and then drizzle it with olive oil. Wrap tightly in clear film (plastic wrap) and stand for 1–2 hours before cutting into slices.

SERVES 3–4

30ml/2 tbsp olive oil
1 large red (bell) pepper, seeded and diced
2.5–5ml/½–1 tsp ground cumin
3 leeks (about 450g/1lb), thinly sliced
150g/5oz baby spinach leaves
45ml/3 tbsp pine nuts, toasted
5 large (US extra large) eggs
15ml/1 tbsp chopped fresh basil
15ml/1 tbsp chopped fresh flat leaf parsley
salt and ground black pepper
watercress, to garnish
50g/2oz/⅔ cup freshly grated Parmesan
  cheese, to serve (optional)

1 Heat a heavy, non-stick frying pan and add the olive oil. Add the diced red pepper and cook over a medium heat, stirring occasionally, for 6–8 minutes, until the pepper is soft and beginning to brown. Add 2.5ml/½ tsp of the ground cumin, mix well and cook for another 1–2 minutes.

2 Stir in the thinly sliced leeks, then partly cover the pan and cook gently for about 5 minutes, or until the leeks have softened and collapsed. Season the cooked vegetables with plenty of salt and ground black pepper.

PAN HAGGERTY

Use a firm-fleshed potato, such as Romano or Maris Piper, which will hold its shape when cooked. For a change, try adding chopped ham or salami between the layers.

SERVES 2

1 large onion
450g/1lb potatoes
30ml/2 tbsp olive oil
25g/1oz/2 tbsp butter
2 garlic cloves, crushed
115g/4oz/1 cup grated mature (sharp)
   Cheddar cheese
45ml/3 tbsp chopped fresh chives, plus
   extra to garnish
salt and ground black pepper

1 Halve and thinly slice the onion. Peel and thinly slice the potatoes.

2 Heat the oil and butter in a large heavy or non-stick frying pan. Remove from the heat and cover the base with a layer of potatoes, followed by layers of onion slices, garlic, cheese, chives and plenty of seasoning.

VARIATIONS
• Other hard cheeses such as Red Leicester or Monterey Jack work well in this recipe.
• For a slightly sweeter flavour and extra colour, use 1 sliced red onion in place of the brown-skinned variety.

3 Continue layering, ending with grated cheese. Cover with a lid or foil and cook the pan haggerty over a gentle heat on the stove top for about 30 minutes, or until the potatoes and onion are tender when tested with a knife.

4 Preheat the grill (broiler) to hot. Uncover the pan, cover the pan handle with foil to protect it, if necessary, and brown the top under the grill. Serve the pan haggerty straight from the pan, sprinkled with extra chives to garnish.

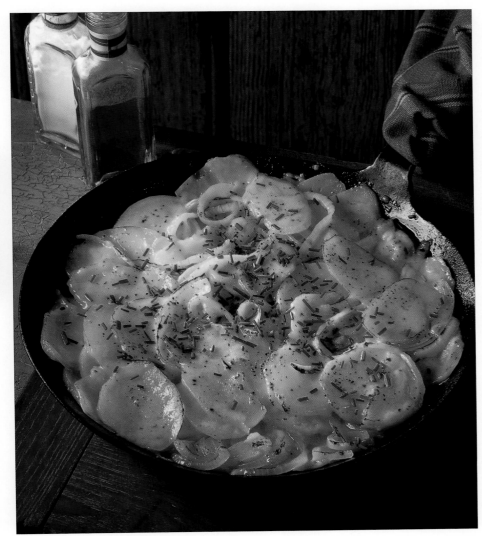

RATATOUILLE

A highly versatile vegetable stew from Provence. Ratatouille is delicious hot or cold, on its own or with eggs, pasta, fish or meat – particularly roast lamb.

SERVES 6

900g/2lb ripe, well-flavoured tomatoes
120ml/4fl oz/½ cup olive oil
2 onions, thinly sliced
2 red (bell) peppers, seeded and
   cut into chunks
1 yellow or orange (bell) pepper,
   seeded and cut into chunks
1 large aubergine (eggplant),
   cut into chunks
2 courgettes (zucchini), cut
   into thick slices
4 garlic cloves, crushed
2 bay leaves
15ml/1 tbsp chopped fresh thyme
salt and ground black pepper

1 To skin the tomatoes plunge them into a bowl of boiling water for about 30 seconds, remove them using a slotted spoon and then refresh in cold water. Peel away the skins and roughly chop the tomato flesh.

2 Heat a little of the oil in a large, heavy pan and fry the onions for 5 minutes. Add the peppers and fry for a further 2 minutes. Drain. Add the aubergine and more oil and fry gently for 5 minutes. Add the remaining oil and courgettes and fry for 3 minutes. Drain.

3 Add the garlic and tomatoes to the pan with the bay leaves and thyme and a little salt and pepper. Cook gently until the tomatoes have softened and are turning pulpy.

4 Return all the vegetables to the pan and cook gently, stirring frequently, for about 15 minutes, until they are fairly pulpy but have retained a little texture. Season with more salt and pepper to taste if required.

COOK'S TIPS

• There are no specific quantities for the vegetables when making ratatouille so you can, to a large extent, vary the quantities and types of vegetables depending on what you have in the refrigerator.
• If the tomatoes are a little tasteless, add 30–45ml/2–3 tbsp tomato purée (paste) and a pinch of sugar to the mixture along with the tomatoes.
• Aubergines no longer need to be salted to draw out the bitter juices, however, this salting process does help prevent the aubergines from soaking up too much oil during frying. So, if you have the time, it is worth sprinkling the aubergine chunks with salt and leaving them in a colander in the sink for about 30 minutes to drain. Rinse them well and pat dry with kitchen paper before frying.

OKRA and TOMATO TAGINE

A spicy vegetarian dish that is delicious served either with other vegetable dishes or as a side dish to accompany a meat tagine.

SERVES 4

350g/12oz small okra
5–6 tomatoes
2 small onions
2 garlic cloves, crushed
1 green chilli, seeded
5ml/1 tsp paprika
a small handful of fresh coriander
    (cilantro) leaves
30ml/2 tbsp vegetable oil
juice of 1 lemon
120ml/4fl oz/½ cup water

1 Preheat the oven to 190°C/350°F/ Gas 5. Trim the okra, then cut the pods into 1cm/½in lengths. Set aside.

2 Peel the tomatoes, remove the seeds, then chop roughly. Set aside. Chop one of the onions, place in a food processor with the garlic, spices and 60ml/4 tbsp water and blend to form a paste.

3 Thinly slice the second onion. Heat the oil in a flameproof casserole or pan and fry the onion for 5–6 minutes until it turns golden brown. Transfer to a plate with a slotted spoon.

4 Reduce the heat and pour the onion and coriander paste over the onions. Cook for 1–2 minutes, stirring frequently, then add the okra, tomatoes and lemon juice. Pour in the water and stir well to mix. Cover tightly and transfer to the oven. Bake for about 15 minutes until the okra is tender.

5 Transfer the tagine to a serving dish, sprinkle with the fried onion rings and serve immediately.

VARIATION
Canned, chopped tomatoes can be used instead of the fresh tomatoes in this recipe – simply add the contents of a 200g/7oz can with the okra in step 4.

JAMAICAN BLACK BEAN POT

Molasses imparts a rich treacly flavour to the spicy sauce, which incorporates a stunning mix of black beans, vibrant red and yellow peppers and orange butternut squash.

SERVES 4

225g/8oz/1¼ cups dried black beans
1 bay leaf
30ml/2 tbsp vegetable oil
1 large onion, chopped
1 garlic clove, chopped
5ml/1 tsp mustard powder
15ml/1 tbsp molasses or black treacle
30ml/2 tbsp soft dark brown sugar
5ml/1 tsp dried thyme
2.5ml/½ tsp dried chilli flakes
5ml/1 tsp vegetable bouillon powder
1 red (bell) pepper, seeded and diced
1 yellow (bell) pepper, seeded
    and diced
675g/1½lb butternut squash or pumpkin,
    seeded and cut into 1cm/½in dice
salt and ground black pepper
sprigs of thyme, to garnish
cornbread or plain boiled rice, to serve

1 Soak the beans overnight in plenty of water, then drain and rinse well. Place in a large pan, cover with fresh water and add the bay leaf. Bring to the boil, then boil rapidly for 10 minutes. Reduce the heat, cover the pan, and simmer for about 30 minutes until tender. Drain, reserving the cooking water. Preheat the oven to 180°C/350°F/Gas 4.

COOK'S TIPS
• To prepare squash or pumpkin, cut it in half using a large sharp knife, then cut off the skin. Remove the seeds using a spoon and cut the flesh into chunks. Choose firm specimens that are blemish-free.
• If you don't have bouillon powder, then dissolve half a stock (bouillon) cube in the bean cooking water.

2 Heat the vegetable oil in a flameproof casserole, add the onion and garlic and sauté for about 5 minutes until softened, stirring occasionally. Stir in the mustard powder, molasses or treacle, sugar, dried thyme, chilli flakes and seasoning. Cook for about 1 minute, stirring, then stir in the black beans.

3 Add enough water to the reserved liquid to make 400ml/14fl oz/1⅔ cups, mix in the bouillon powder and pour into the casserole. Bake for 25 minutes.

4 Add the peppers and the squash or pumpkin and mix well. Cover, then bake for 45 minutes. Garnish with thyme.

VEGETABLE KORMA

The blending of spices is an ancient art in India. Here the aim is to produce a subtle, aromatic curry rather than an assault on the senses.

SERVES 4

50g/2oz/¼ cup butter
2 onions, sliced
2 garlic cloves, crushed
2.5cm/1in piece fresh root ginger, grated
5ml/1 tsp ground cumin
15ml/1 tbsp ground coriander
6 cardamom pods
5cm/2in piece of cinnamon stick
5ml/1 tsp ground turmeric
1 fresh red chilli, seeded and
    finely chopped
1 potato, peeled and cut into
    2.5cm/1in cubes
1 small aubergine (eggplant), chopped
115g/4oz/1½ cups mushrooms,
    thickly sliced
175ml/6fl oz/¾ cup water
115g/4oz/1 cup green beans, cut into
    2.5cm/1in lengths
60ml/4 tbsp natural (plain) yogurt
150ml/¼ pint/⅔ cup double (heavy) cream
5ml/1 tsp garam masala
salt and ground black pepper
fresh coriander (cilantro) sprigs, to garnish
boiled rice and poppadums, to serve

1 Melt the butter in a heavy pan. Add the onions and cook for 5 minutes until soft. Add the garlic and ginger and cook for 2 minutes, then stir in the cumin, coriander, cardamom pods, cinnamon stick, turmeric and finely chopped chilli. Cook, stirring constantly, for 30 seconds.

VARIATION

All kinds of vegetables and pulses can be used for this korma; try broccoli, carrots, cauliflower, peas, canned or fresh beans and canned chickpeas.

2 Add the potato cubes, aubergine and mushrooms and the water. Cover the pan, bring to the boil, then lower the heat and simmer for 15 minutes. Add the beans and cook, uncovered, for 5 minutes. With a slotted spoon, remove the vegetables to a warmed serving dish and keep hot.

3 Allow the cooking liquid to bubble up until it has reduced a little. Season with salt and pepper, then stir in the yogurt, cream and garam masala. Pour the sauce over the vegetables and garnish with fresh coriander. Serve with boiled rice and poppadums.

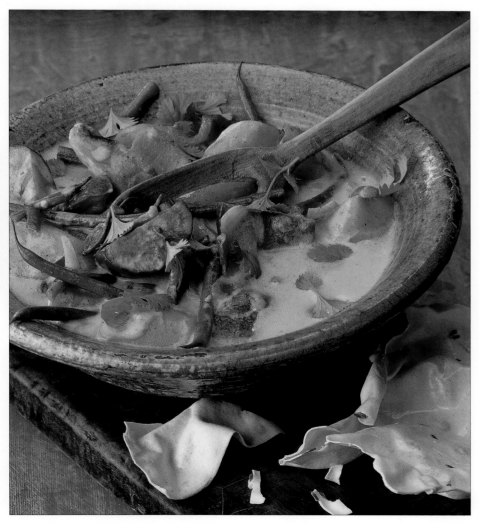

TOFU and VEGETABLE THAI CURRY

Traditional Thai ingredients – chillies, galangal, lemon grass and kaffir lime leaves – give this curry a wonderfully fragrant aroma.

SERVES 4

175g/6oz tofu, drained
45ml/3 tbsp dark soy sauce
15ml/1 tbsp sesame oil
5ml/1 tsp chilli sauce
2.5cm/1in piece fresh root ginger,
   finely grated
225g/8oz cauliflower
225g/8oz broccoli
30ml/2 tbsp vegetable oil
1 onion, sliced
400ml/14fl oz/1⅔ cups coconut milk
150ml/¼ pint/⅔ cup water
1 red (bell) pepper, seeded
   and chopped
175g/6oz green beans, halved
115g/4oz/1½ cups shiitake or button
   (white) mushrooms, halved
shredded spring onions (scallions),
   to garnish
boiled jasmine rice or noodles,
   to serve

For the curry paste
2 chillies, seeded and chopped
1 lemon grass stalk, chopped
2.5cm/1in piece fresh galangal, chopped
2 kaffir lime leaves
10ml/2 tsp ground coriander
a few sprigs fresh coriander (cilantro),
   including the stalks

1 Cut the drained tofu into 2.5cm/1in cubes and place in an ovenproof dish. Mix together the soy sauce, sesame oil, chilli sauce and ginger and pour over the tofu. Toss gently to coat all the cubes evenly, then leave to marinate for at least 2 hours or overnight if possible, turning and basting the tofu occasionally.

2 To make the curry paste, place the chopped chillies, lemon grass, galangal, kaffir lime leaves, ground coriander and fresh coriander in a food processor and process for a few seconds until well blended. Add 45ml/3 tbsp water and process to a thick paste.

3 Preheat the oven to 190°C/375°F/Gas 5. Using a large sharp knife, cut the cauliflower and broccoli into small florets and cut any stalks into thin slices.

4 Heat the vegetable oil in a frying pan, add the sliced onion and gently fry for about 8 minutes, or until soft and lightly browned. Stir in the prepared curry paste and the coconut milk. Add the water and bring to the boil.

5 Stir in the red pepper, green beans, cauliflower and broccoli. Transfer to a Chinese sand pot or earthenware casserole. Cover and place in the oven.

6 Stir the tofu and marinade, then place the dish in the top of the oven and cook for 30 minutes, then stir them into the curry with the mushrooms. Reduce the oven temperature to 180°C/350°F/Gas 4 and cook for about 15 minutes, or until the vegetables are tender. Garnish with spring onions and serve with boiled jasmine rice or noodles.

COOK'S TIP
Tofu or beancurd is made from soya beans and is sold in blocks. It is a creamy white colour and has a solid gel-like texture. Tofu has a bland flavour and its absorbent nature means that it takes on the flavours of marinades or any other food that it is cooked with.

BASMATI RICE and NUT PILAFF

Vegetarians will love this simple pilaff. Add wild or cultivated mushrooms, if you like.

SERVES 4

15–30ml/1–2 tbsp sunflower oil
1 onion, chopped
1 garlic clove, crushed
1 large carrot, coarsely grated
225g/8oz/generous 1 cup basmati
   rice, soaked
5ml/1 tsp cumin seeds
10ml/2 tsp ground coriander
10ml/2 tsp black mustard seeds (optional)
4 green cardamom pods
450ml/¾ pint/scant 2 cups vegetable
   stock or water
1 bay leaf
75g/3oz/½ cup shelled walnuts and/or
   unsalted cashew nuts
salt and ground black pepper
fresh parsley or coriander (cilantro)
   sprigs, to garnish

1 Heat the oil in a large frying pan. Add the onion, garlic and carrot and cook for 3–4 minutes, stirring occasionally.

2 Drain the rice and add it to the pan with the cumin seeds, ground coriander, black mustard seeds, if using, and the green cardamom pods. Cook for about 1 minute, stirring to coat the grains in oil.

3 Pour in the vegetable stock or water, add the bay leaf and season well with salt and pepper. Bring to the boil, then lower the heat, cover and simmer very gently for 10–12 minutes.

4 Remove the frying pan from the heat without lifting the lid. Leave to stand in a warm place for about 5 minutes, then check the rice. If it is cooked, there will be small steam holes on the surface of the rice. Remove the bay leaf and the cardamom pods.

5 Stir the walnuts and/or cashew nuts into the rice mixture. Taste to check the seasoning and add more salt and pepper if necessary. Spoon into warmed individual bowls or on to a large platter, garnish with the sprigs of fresh parsley or coriander and serve immediately.

COOK'S TIPS
• Use whichever nuts you prefer in this pilaff – even unsalted peanuts taste good – although almonds, brazil nuts, cashew nuts or pistachio nuts add a slightly more exotic flavour.
• If you don't have basmati rice, then use any other long grain rice. Thai jasmine rice has a particularly good flavour.

VEGETABLE COUSCOUS with SAFFRON and HARISSA

This spicy, north African dish makes an excellent main meal, or serve as part of a vegetarian buffet.

SERVES 4

45ml/3 tbsp olive oil
1 onion, chopped
2 garlic cloves, crushed
5ml/1 tsp ground cumin
5ml/1 tsp paprika
400g/14oz can chopped tomatoes
300ml/½ pint/1¼ cups vegetable stock
1 cinnamon stick
generous pinch of saffron threads
4 baby aubergines (eggplant), quartered
8 baby courgettes (zucchini), trimmed
8 baby carrots
225g/8oz/1⅓ cups couscous
425g/15oz can chickpeas, drained
175g/6oz/¾ cup pitted prunes
45ml/3 tbsp chopped fresh parsley
45ml/3 tbsp chopped fresh coriander
10–15ml/2–3 tsp harissa
salt

1 Heat the olive oil in a large pan. Add the onion and garlic and cook gently for 5 minutes until soft. Add the cumin and paprika and cook, stirring, for 1 minute.

2 Add the tomatoes, stock, cinnamon stick, saffron, aubergines, courgettes and carrots, and season with salt. Bring to the boil, cover, lower the heat and cook gently for 20 minutes until the vegetables are just tender.

3 Line a steamer or colander with a double thickness of muslin (cheesecloth). Soak the couscous according to the instructions on the packet.

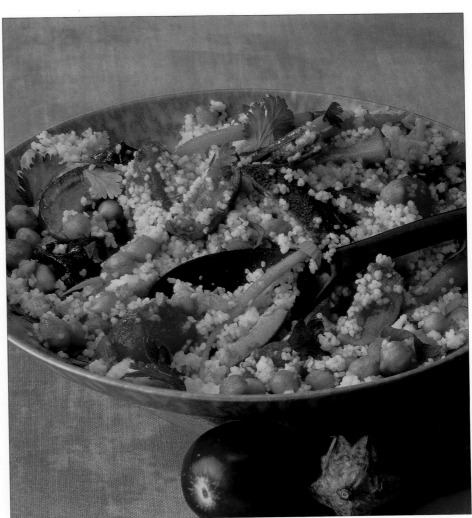

COOK'S TIPS
• Couscous is made from durum wheat and has a similar appearance to semolina. It has a very mild flavour and takes on the flavour of any ingredients it is mixed with. Most couscous is sold pre-cooked and only needs to be re-hydrated in boiling water or according to packet instructions.
• Harissa is a spicy paste made from red chillies, coriander, caraway, garlic, salt and olive oil. Its bright red/orange colour is an indicator of its fiery flavour. It is sold in cans, jars and tubes.

4 Add the chickpeas and prunes to the vegetables, stir and cook for 5 minutes.

5 Spread the couscous in the prepared steamer. Place the steamer on top of the vegetables, cover and cook for 5 minutes until the couscous is hot.

6 Stir the herbs into the vegetables. Heap the couscous on to a serving dish. Using a slotted spoon, remove the vegetables from the frying pan and add to the couscous. Spoon over a little sauce and toss gently. Stir the harissa into the remaining sauce and serve separately.

BUCKWHEAT NOODLES with CABBAGE, POTATOES and CHEESE

This is a very unusual pasta dish from Valtellina in the Italian Alps. The pale brown buckwheat noodles called pizzoccheri are unique to this area.

SERVES 6

400g/14oz Savoy cabbage, cut into
　1cm/½in strips
2 potatoes, total weight about 200g/7oz,
　cut into 5mm/¼in slices
400g/14oz dried pizzoccheri
　(buckwheat noodles)
75g/3oz/6 tbsp butter
1 generous bunch fresh sage
　leaves, shredded
2 garlic cloves
200g/7oz Fontina cheese, rind removed
　and thinly sliced
30–45ml/2–3 tbsp freshly grated
　Parmesan cheese, plus extra to serve
salt and ground black pepper

COOK'S TIPS
• Look for packets of dried pizzoccheri
pasta in Italian delicatessens.
• Fontina is an Italian mountain cheese
with a sweet, nutty taste. If you cannot
get it, look for Taleggio, Gruyère or
Emmenthal – they are all similar cheeses.

1 Bring a very large pan of salted water
to the boil. Add the cabbage strips and
potato slices and boil for 5 minutes.

2 Add the pasta to the pan, stir well and
let the water return to the boil over a
high heat. Lower the heat and simmer
for about 15 minutes, or according to
the instructions on the packet, until the
pasta is just tender.

3 Drain the pasta and vegetables and
set aside. Melt the butter in the pan.
Add the sage and whole garlic cloves
and fry over a low to medium heat until
the garlic is golden and sizzling. Lift the
garlic out of the pan and discard it. Set
the sage and garlic butter aside.

4 Pour one-quarter of the pasta and
vegetable mixture into a warmed large
bowl and arrange about one-third of
the Fontina slices on top. Repeat these
layers until all the ingredients have been
used, then sprinkle with the grated
Parmesan. Pour the sage and garlic
butter over the top and serve
immediately, with extra grated Parmesan
handed separately.

VARIATION
You could use chard or spinach instead
of the cabbage. Spinach will need much
less cooking, so add it to the pan about
5 minutes before the end of the cooking
time in step 2.

FETTUCINE with BUTTER and PARMESAN

Very few ingredients are needed to make up this incredibly simple dish. It comes from northern Italy, where butter and cheeses are the most popular ingredients for serving with pasta. This dish is especially popular with children.

SERVES 4

400g/14oz fresh or dried fettucine
50g/2oz/¼ cup unsalted (sweet)
　butter, cubed
115g/4oz/1¼ cups freshly grated
　Parmesan cheese
salt and ground black pepper

VARIATIONS
• Other long pastas would be just as good
in this recipe; try spaghetti, linguine or
tagliatelle. Spinach or tomato flavoured
versions would also work well.
• Try freshly grated Pecorino cheese
instead of the Parmesan.

1 Cook the pasta in a large pan of
salted boiling water until just tender, or
according to the instructions on the
packet. Drain thoroughly, then tip the
pasta into a large warmed bowl.

2 Add the cubes of butter and the
grated Parmesan, one-third at a time,
tossing the pasta after each addition until
it is evenly coated. Season to taste and
serve immediately.

PASTA TWISTS with PESTO

Bottled pesto is a useful stand-by, but if you have a food processor or blender, it is very easy to make a delicious home-made version.

SERVES 4

50g/2oz fresh basil leaves, plus extra fresh
    basil leaves, to garnish
2–4 garlic cloves
60ml/4 tbsp pine nuts
120ml/4fl oz/½ cup extra virgin
    olive oil
115g/4oz/1¼ cups freshly grated Parmesan
    cheese, plus extra to serve
25g/1oz/¼ cup freshly grated
    Pecorino cheese
400g/14oz/3½ cups dried pasta
    twists (fusilli)
salt and ground black pepper

1 Put the basil, garlic and pine nuts in a food processor. Add 60ml/4 tbsp of the oil. Process until chopped, then stop the machine and scrape the bowl.

2 Turn the machine on again and slowly add the remaining olive oil in a thin, steady stream through the feeder tube. You may need to stop the machine and scrape down the sides of the bowl once or twice to make sure that everything is evenly mixed.

3 Scrape the mixture into a large bowl and beat in the cheeses with a wooden spoon. Taste and add salt and ground black pepper if necessary.

4 Cook the pasta in a large pan of salted boiling water for 10 minutes, or according to the instructions on the packet, until just tender. Drain the pasta well, then add it to the bowl of pesto and toss well. Serve immediately, garnished with the extra fresh basil leaves. Hand around the extra shaved Parmesan separately.

COOK'S TIP

Fresh pesto can be made up to 2–3 days in advance. To store it, transfer the pesto to a small bowl and pour a thin film of olive oil over the surface. Cover the bowl tightly with clear film (plastic wrap) and keep it in the refrigerator.

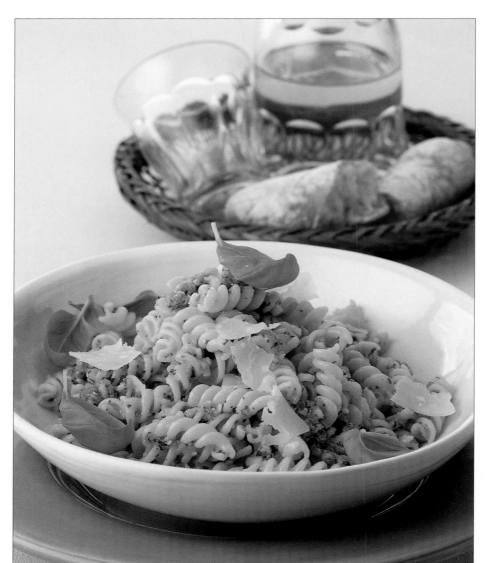

PASTA with CHEESE and CREAM

The Italian name for this dish – Mezzanotte – means middle of the night, which is when this rich and filling dish is eaten – after a night on the tiles. When you arrive home hungry from a party, it's just the thing to sober you up!

SERVES 4

400g/14oz/3½ cups dried rigatoni
3 egg yolks
105ml/7 tbsp grated Parmesan cheese
200g/7oz/scant 1 cup ricotta cheese
60ml/4 tbsp double (heavy) cream
nutmeg
40g/1½oz/3 tbsp butter
salt and ground black pepper

1 Cook the pasta according to the instructions on the packet.

2 Meanwhile, mix the egg yolks, grated Parmesan and ricotta together in a bowl. Add the cream and mix with a fork.

3 Grate in nutmeg to taste, then season with plenty of black pepper and a little salt. Drain the pasta thoroughly when cooked. Return the clean pan to the heat. Melt the butter, add the drained pasta and toss over a medium heat.

4 Turn off the heat under the pan and add the ricotta mixture. Stir well with a large spoon for 10–15 seconds, or until all the pasta is coated in sauce. Serve immediately, in warmed individual bowls with plenty of ground black pepper.

SPAGHETTI with BUTTER and HERBS

This is a versatile recipe. You can use just one favourite herb or several – basil, flat leaf parsley, rosemary, thyme, marjoram or sage would all work well.

SERVES 4

400g/14oz fresh or dried spaghetti
   alla chitarra
2 good handfuls mixed fresh herbs,
   plus extra herb leaves and flowers
   to garnish
115g/4oz/½ cup butter, diced
salt and ground black pepper
freshly grated Parmesan cheese, to serve

1 Cook the pasta in a large pan of salted boiling water for 10–12 minutes until just tender or according to the instructions on the packet.

2 Using a large sharp knife, chop the fresh herbs roughly or finely, whichever you prefer.

COOK'S TIP
Square-shaped chitarra spaghetti is the traditional type for this sauce, but you can use any type of long thin pasta, such as ordinary spaghetti or spaghettini, or even linguine.

VARIATION
If you like the flavour of garlic, add one or two crushed cloves to the pan when melting the butter.

3 Drain the pasta in a colander and then return the pasta to the pan. Add the butter and heat until it melts and sizzles, then add the chopped herbs and salt and pepper to taste.

4 Toss the pasta over a medium heat until it is thoroughly coated in the butter and herbs.

5 Serve the pasta immediately in warmed shallow bowls, sprinkled with some extra herb leaves and flowers. Hand around a bowl of freshly grated Parmesan separately.

SPAGHETTI with CHEESE and BLACK PEPPER

This dish is very quick and easy to cook, perfect for a midweek supper. The flavours are very simple, so choose a strong-tasting cheese and a good extra virgin olive oil. Pecorino is traditional in this dish, but Parmesan could also be used.

SERVES 4

400g/14oz fresh or
   dried spaghetti
115g/4oz/1 cup freshly grated
   Pecorino cheese
about 5ml/1 tsp coarsely ground
   black pepper
extra virgin olive oil, to taste
salt

1 Cook the fresh or dried pasta in a large pan of salted boiling water until it is just tender, or according to the instructions on the packet.

2 As soon as the spaghetti is cooked, drain it, leaving it a little moister than usual, then tip the spaghetti straight into a large warmed serving bowl.

3 Add the freshly grated cheese, lots of black pepper, and salt to taste. Toss the pasta well to mix, then moisten with as much olive oil as you like. Serve the pasta immediately.

SPAGHETTI with ROCKET PESTO

This is the pesto for real rocket lovers. It is sharp and peppery, and delicious for a summer pasta meal with a glass of chilled dry white wine.

SERVES 4

4 garlic cloves
90ml/6 tbsp pine nuts
2 large handfuls of rocket (arugula), total weight about 150g/5oz, stalks removed
50g/2oz/⅔ cup freshly grated Parmesan cheese
50g/2oz/⅔ cup freshly grated Pecorino cheese
90ml/6 tbsp extra virgin olive oil
400g/14oz fresh or dried spaghetti
salt and ground black pepper
freshly grated Parmesan and Pecorino cheese, to serve

1 Put the garlic and pine nuts in a food processor or blender and process until finely chopped. Add the rocket, grated Parmesan and Pecorino, and olive oil.

2 Add salt and pepper, to taste and process for 5 seconds. Stop and scrape down the side of the bowl, then process for 5–10 seconds more until a smooth paste is formed.

3 Cook the spaghetti in a large pan of boiling salted water until just tender, or according to the packet instructions.

4 Spoon the pesto into a large mixing bowl. Just before the pasta is ready, add one or two ladlefuls of the cooking water to the pesto and stir well to mix.

5 Drain the pasta, tip it into the bowl of pesto and toss well to mix. Serve immediately, with the grated cheeses handed separately.

VARIATION
To temper the flavour of the rocket and make the pesto milder, add 115g/4oz/ ½ cup ricotta or mascarpone cheese to the pesto in step 4 and mix well before adding the water.

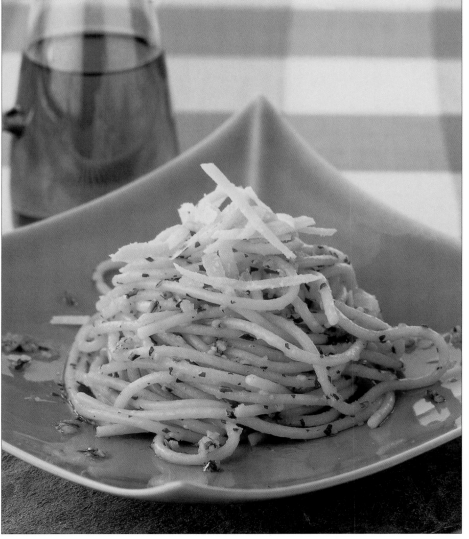

PASTA SHELLS with TOMATOES and RICOTTA

Nothing could be more simple than hot pasta tossed with fresh ripe tomatoes, ricotta cheese and sweet basil. Serve it on hot summer days — it is surprisingly refreshing.

SERVES 4–6

350g/12oz/3 cups dried conchiglie
130g/4½oz/generous ½ cup ricotta cheese
6 ripe plum tomatoes, diced
2 garlic cloves, crushed
a handful of fresh basil leaves, shredded,
  plus extra basil leaves to garnish
60ml/4 tbsp extra virgin olive oil
salt and ground black pepper

1 Cook the pasta in boiling salted water according to the packet instructions.

VARIATIONS

• Use diced mozzarella instead of ricotta.
• An avocado is the ideal ingredient for adding extra colour and flavour to this pasta dish. Halve, stone (pit) and peel, then dice the flesh. Toss it with the hot pasta at the last minute.

2 Meanwhile, put the ricotta cheese in a large mixing bowl and mash with a fork until soft and creamy.

3 Add the diced tomatoes (see Cook's Tip), crushed garlic and shredded basil to the softened ricotta cheese, with salt and pepper to taste, and mix well. Add the olive oil and whisk thoroughly. Taste for seasoning.

4 Drain the cooked pasta, tip it into the ricotta and tomato mixture and toss well to mix. Garnish with basil leaves and serve immediately, sprinkled with black pepper.

COOK'S TIP

If you like, skin the tomatoes before you dice them by plunging them into boiling water for 30 seconds and then refresh in cold water before peeling.

LINGUINE with ROCKET

You'll find this dish served as a first course in many a fashionable restaurant in Italy. It is very quick and easy to make at home and is worth trying for yourself.

SERVES 2

350g/12oz fresh or dried linguine
120ml/4fl oz/½ cup extra virgin olive oil
1 large bunch rocket (arugula), about
    150g/5oz, stalks removed, shredded
    or torn
75g/3oz/1 cup freshly grated
    Parmesan cheese
salt and ground black pepper

VARIATION
Oil-based pasta sauces such as this one are best served with fine, long pastas such as linguine. Spaghetti, capelli d'angelo, bucatini or fettucine would work just as well in this recipe.

1 Cook the pasta in a large pan of salted boiling water for 8–10 minutes until it is just tender, or according to the instructions on the packet. As soon as the pasta is cooked, drain thoroughly.

2 Heat about 60ml/4 tbsp of the olive oil in the pasta pan, then add the drained pasta, followed by the rocket. Toss over a medium to high heat for 1–2 minutes or until the rocket is just wilted, then remove the pan from the heat.

3 Tip the pasta and rocket into a warmed, large serving bowl. Add half the freshly grated Parmesan cheese and the remaining olive oil. Add a little salt and black pepper to taste.

4 Toss the mixture quickly to mix and serve immediately. Hand round the remaining Parmesan cheese.

COOK'S TIP
Buy rocket by the bunch from the greengrocer. The type sold in small cellophane packets in supermarkets is usually very expensive. Always check when buying rocket that all the leaves are bright green. In hot weather, rocket leaves quickly turn yellow.

SPAGHETTI with GARLIC and OIL

This simple Roman pasta dish can be made in less than 15 minutes. Use fresh chillies if you prefer and, since the oil is so important, the very best extra virgin olive oil.

SERVES 4

400g/14oz fresh or dried spaghetti
90ml/6 tbsp extra virgin olive oil
2–4 garlic cloves, crushed
I dried red chilli
I small handful fresh flat leaf parsley,
  roughly chopped
salt

COOK'S TIP
Don't use salt when you are preparing the hot oil, garlic and chilli mixture, because the salt will not dissolve sufficiently. This is why plenty of salt is recommended for cooking the pasta.

I Cook the pasta in a large pan of salted boiling water, according to the packet instructions, until it is just tender, adding plenty of salt to the water (see Cook's Tip).

2 When the pasta is just tender, drain it by tipping it into a large colander, then transfer it to a warmed, large serving bowl. Rinse out the pasta pan and dry.

3 Heat the olive oil in the pan. Add the crushed garlic and the whole dried chilli and stir over a low heat for a minute or two until the garlic is just beginning to brown. Remove the chilli and discard.

4 Pour the hot olive oil and cooked garlic mixture over the pasta, add the roughly chopped fresh flat leaf parsley and toss vigorously until the pasta glistens, then serve immediately.

SIDE DISHES

With the modern emphasis on eating plenty of
vegetables, serving several side dishes makes sense,
but it can present logistical problems. Space on top
of the stove is often limited, so use the oven as
well. Choose something quick and simple, such as
Cauliflower with Tomatoes and Cumin, Courgettes
in Tomato Sauce or Roasted Tomatoes and Garlic.
Or go for a dish that's a little out-of-the-ordinary,
such as Baked Fennel with a Crumb Crust, Spinach
with Sweet Potatoes, or Roasted Potatoes
with Garlic and Red Onions.

BRAISED CARROTS with LEEKS

Sweet carrots and leeks go well together and are good finished with a little chopped mint, chervil or parsley. This is a good accompaniment to roast beef, lamb or chicken.

SERVES 4

65g/2½oz/5 tbsp butter
675g/1½lb carrots, thickly sliced
a little sugar
2 fresh bay leaves
75ml/5 tbsp water
675g/1½lb leeks, cut into 5cm/2in lengths
120ml/4fl oz/½ cup white wine
30ml/2 tbsp chopped fresh mint, chervil
　or parsley
salt and ground black pepper

1 Melt 25g/1oz/2 tbsp of the butter in a wide, heavy pan and cook the carrots without allowing them to brown, for about 5 minutes. Add the bay leaves, seasoning, sugar and the water. Bring to the boil, cover and cook for 10 minutes, or until the carrots are just tender.

2 Uncover the pan and boil until the juices have evaporated, leaving the carrots moist and glazed. Remove the carrots from the pan and set aside.

3 Melt 25g/1oz/2 tbsp of the remaining butter in the pan. Add the leeks and fry them over a low heat for 4–5 minutes, without allowing them to brown.

4 Add seasoning, a good pinch of sugar, the wine and half the chopped herbs. Heat until simmering, then cover and cook gently for 5–8 minutes, until the leeks are tender, but not collapsed.

5 Uncover the leeks and turn them in the buttery juices. Increase the heat and then boil the liquid rapidly until it is reduced to a few tablespoons.

6 Add the carrots to the leeks and reheat them gently, stirring occasionally, then add the remaining butter. Adjust the seasoning, if necessary. Transfer to a warmed serving dish and serve sprinkled with the remaining chopped herbs.

VARIATION
Braised leeks in tarragon cream
Cook 900g/2lb leeks, cut into 5cm/2in lengths, in 40g/1½oz/3 tbsp butter as step 3. Season with salt and pepper, add a pinch of sugar, 45ml/3 tbsp tarragon vinegar, 6 fresh tarragon sprigs or 5ml/1 tsp dried tarragon and 60ml/4 tbsp white wine. Cover and cook as step 4. Add 150ml/¼ pint/⅔ cup double (heavy) cream and allow to bubble and thicken. Adjust the seasoning and serve sprinkled with plenty of finely chopped fresh tarragon leaves. A spoonful of tarragon-flavoured mustard is good stirred into these creamy leeks. Serve with fish or chicken dishes.

BABY LEEKS in RED WINE with AROMATICS

Coriander seeds and oregano lend a Greek flavour to this dish of braised leeks. Serve it as part of a mixed hors d'oeuvre or as a partner for baked white fish.

SERVES 6

12 baby leeks or 6 thick leeks
15ml/1 tbsp coriander seeds,
   lightly crushed
5cm/2in piece of cinnamon stick
120ml/4fl oz/½ cup olive oil
3 fresh bay leaves
2 strips pared orange rind
5–6 fresh or dried oregano sprigs
5ml/1 tsp sugar
150ml/¼ pint/⅔ cup fruity red wine
10ml/2 tsp balsamic or
   sherry vinegar
30ml/2 tbsp coarsely chopped fresh
   oregano or marjoram
salt and ground black pepper

1 For baby leeks, simply trim the ends, but leave them whole. If you are using thicker leeks, cut them into 5–7.5cm/ 2–3in lengths.

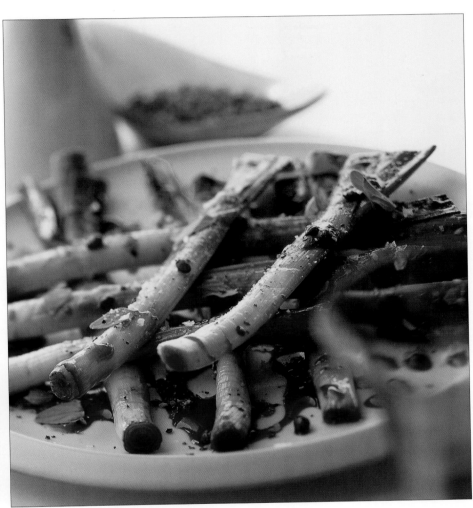

2 Place the coriander seeds and cinnamon in a pan wide enough to take all the leeks in a single layer. Cook over a medium heat for 2–3 minutes, until the spices give off a fragrant aroma, then stir in the olive oil, bay leaves, orange rind, fresh or dried oregano, sugar, wine and balsamic or sherry vinegar. Bring to the boil and simmer for 5 minutes.

3 Add the leeks to the pan. Bring back to the boil, reduce the heat and cover the pan. Cook the leeks gently for 5 minutes. Uncover and simmer gently for another 5–8 minutes, until the leeks are just tender when tested with the tip of a sharp knife.

4 Use a slotted spoon to transfer the leeks to a serving dish. Boil the pan juices rapidly until reduced to about 75–90ml/5–6 tbsp. Add salt and pepper to taste and pour the liquid over the leeks. Leave to cool.

5 The leeks can be left to stand for several hours. If you chill them, bring them back to room temperature again before serving. Sprinkle the chopped herbs over the leeks just before serving.

COOK'S TIP
Genuine balsamic vinegar from Modena in northern Italy has been produced for over 1,000 years. It has a high sugar content and wonderfully strong bouquet. It is a very dark brown colour and has a deep, rich flavour with hints of herbs and port. Nowadays you can find quite good balsamic vinegar in supermarkets. It is expensive, but the flavour is so rich that you only need to use a little.

BRAISED LETTUCE and PEAS with MINT

Based on the traditional French way of braising peas with lettuce in butter, this dish is delicious with simply cooked fish or roast or grilled duck.

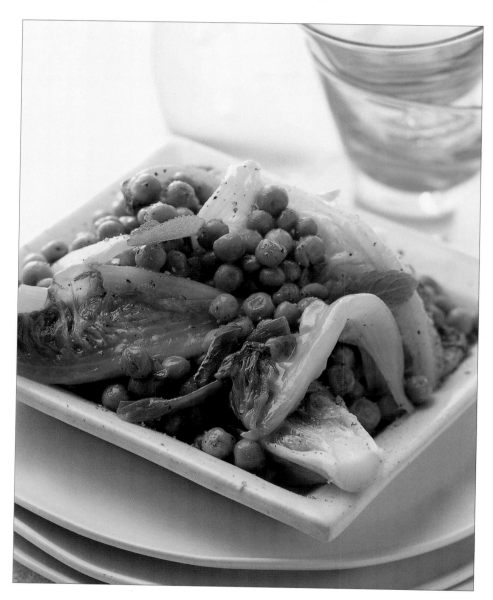

2 Toss the vegetables in the butter, then sprinkle in the sugar, 2.5ml/½ tsp salt and plenty of black pepper. Cover, then cook very gently for 5 minutes, stirring once.

3 Add the peas and mint sprigs to the pan. Toss the peas in the buttery juices, then pour in the light stock or water.

4 Cover the pan and cook over a gentle heat for a further 5 minutes until the peas are almost tender, then remove the lid from the pan. Increase the heat to high and cook, stirring occasionally, until the cooking liquid has reduced to a few tablespoons.

5 Stir in the remaining butter and adjust the seasoning. Transfer to a warmed serving dish and garnish with the extra mint. Serve immediately.

VARIATIONS

• Braise about 250g/9oz baby carrots with the lettuce.
• Use 1 lettuce, shredding it coarsely, and omit the fresh mint. Towards the end of cooking, stir in about 150g/5oz rocket (arugula) – preferably the slightly stronger-flavoured, wild variety – and cook briefly until just wilted.
• Fry 115g/4oz chopped smoked bacon or pancetta with 1 small chopped red or white onion in the butter. Use 1 bunch of spring onions and omit the mint. Stir in some chopped fresh flat leaf parsley before serving. This version is also very good with small, white summer turnips, braised with the lettuce.

SERVES 4

50g/2oz/¼ cup butter
4 Little Gem (Bibb) lettuces,
    halved lengthwise
2 bunches spring onions (scallions)
5ml/1 tsp sugar
400g/14oz shelled peas (about
    1kg/2¼lb in pods)
a few sprigs of mint, plus extra fresh mint
    to garnish
120ml/4fl oz/½ cup light vegetable or
    chicken stock or water
salt and ground black pepper

1 Melt half the butter in a wide, heavy pan over a low heat. Add the lettuces and spring onions.

SPINACH with SWEET POTATOES

Sweet potatoes make an interesting alternative to the ordinary variety. Here the garlic and ginger subtly complement the flavours of the potatoes and spinach.

SERVES 4

30ml/2 tbsp sunflower oil
I onion, chopped
I garlic clove, finely chopped
2.5cm/Iin piece fresh root ginger,
    peeled and grated
2.5ml/½ tsp cayenne pepper
675g/I½lb sweet potatoes
150ml/¼ pint/⅔ cup vegetable or
    chicken stock
225g/8oz spinach
45ml/3 tbsp pine nuts, toasted
salt and ground black pepper

I Soak a clay potato pot in cold water for 20 minutes, then drain. Heat the oil in a large frying pan, add the onion, garlic, ginger and cayenne pepper and fry gently, stirring occasionally, for about 8 minutes, or until the onion is softened.

2 Peel the sweet potatoes and cut them into 2.5cm/Iin chunks. Add the chunks to the frying pan and stir to coat them in the oil and spices.

COOK'S TIPS
• If you don't have a clay pot, use a deep baking dish – you won't need to soak it.
• To toast pine nuts, cook them for 3–4 minutes in a heavy pan, until they turn golden brown. Stir them occasionally and take care not to burn them.

VARIATIONS
• Add a drained, 400g/14oz can chickpeas to the potato mixture after 30 minutes cooking and stir well.
• Use baby new potatoes in place of the sweet potatoes.

3 Transfer the potato mixture to the clay pot and add the stock. Cover the pot and place in an unheated oven. Set the oven to 220°C/425°F/Gas 7 and cook for 50–60 minutes, or until the potatoes are just tender, stirring halfway through cooking.

4 Wash the spinach and shred roughly. Stir into the potatoes with the toasted pine nuts, re-cover the clay pot and cook for a further 5 minutes in the oven. Remove from the oven and leave to stand for 5 minutes. Adjust the seasoning and serve immediately.

CAULIFLOWER with TOMATOES and CUMIN

This makes an excellent side dish to serve with grilled meat or fish.

SERVES 4

30ml/2 tbsp sunflower or olive oil
1 onion, chopped
1 garlic clove, crushed
1 small cauliflower, broken into florets
5ml/1 tsp cumin seeds
good pinch of ground ginger
4 tomatoes, peeled, seeded
    and quartered
175ml/6fl oz/¾ cup water
15–30ml/1–2 tbsp lemon juice (optional)
salt and ground black pepper
30ml/2 tbsp chopped fresh coriander
    (cilantro) (optional)

VARIATIONS

• Use a 200g/7oz can of chopped
tomatoes instead of the fresh tomatoes.
• Broccoli florets can be used in place of
the cauliflower, if you prefer.

1 Heat the oil in a flameproof casserole, add the onion and garlic and stir-fry for 2–3 minutes until the onion is softened. Add the cauliflower and stir-fry for a further 2–3 minutes until the cauliflower is flecked with brown. Add the cumin seeds and ginger, and fry briskly for 1 minute, then add the peeled, seeded and quartered tomatoes, the water and some salt and pepper to taste.

2 Bring to the boil, then reduce the heat, cover with a plate or with foil and simmer for 6–7 minutes, or until the cauliflower is just tender.

3 Stir in a little lemon juice to sharpen the flavour, if you like, and adjust the seasoning if necessary. Sprinkle over the chopped fresh coriander, if using, and serve immediately.

ROAST VEGETABLES with FRESH HERBS and CHILLI SAUCE

Oven roasting brings out all the flavours of these classic Mediterranean vegetables. Serve them hot with grilled or roast meat or fish.

SERVES 4

2–3 courgettes (zucchini)
1 large onion
1 red (bell) pepper
16 cherry tomatoes
2 garlic cloves, chopped
pinch of cumin seeds
5ml/1 tsp fresh thyme or 4–5 torn
    basil leaves
60ml/4 tbsp olive oil
juice of ½ lemon
5–10ml/1–2 tsp harissa
fresh thyme sprigs, to garnish

COOK'S TIP

To make fresh harissa, soak 6 seeded red chillies in warm water until soft. Drain and blend with 2 crushed garlic cloves, 2.5ml/ ½ tsp sea salt, 5ml/1 tsp ground cumin, 2.5ml/½ tsp ground coriander and 120ml/ 4fl oz/½ cup olive oil. Process until smooth. Any unused paste should be refrigerated.

1 Preheat the oven to 220°C/425°F/ Gas 7. Trim the courgettes and then cut them into long thin strips. Cut the onion into thin wedges and cut the pepper into fairly large chunks, discarding the seeds and core.

VARIATION

Other vegetables would work well in this dish. Add wedges of red and yellow (bell) peppers in place of one of the courgettes, or add chunks of aubergine (eggplant).

2 Place the vegetables in a large roasting pan, add the tomatoes, chopped garlic, cumin seeds and thyme or basil. Sprinkle with the olive oil and toss to coat. Cook in the oven for 25–30 minutes until the vegetables are very soft and slightly charred at the edges.

3 Blend the lemon juice with the harissa and stir into the roasted vegetables just before serving, garnished with the fresh thyme sprigs.

ROASTED TOMATOES and GARLIC

*These are so simple to prepare yet taste absolutely wonderful. Use a large, shallow
earthenware dish that will allow the tomatoes to sear and char in a very hot oven.*

SERVES 4

8 well-flavoured tomatoes (see Cook's
   Tip), halved
12 garlic cloves, unpeeled
60ml/4 tbsp extra virgin olive oil
3–4 bay leaves
salt and ground black pepper
45ml/3 tbsp fresh oregano leaves,
   to garnish

COOK'S TIP
If possible use ripe plum tomatoes for
this recipe as they not only keep their
shape and their delicious flavour, but also
do not fall apart when roasted at such a
high temperature. Leave the stalks on the
tomatoes, if you like.

1 Preheat the oven to 230°C/450°F/
Gas 8. Select a large, shallow ovenproof
dish that will hold all the tomato halves
snugly in a single layer. Arrange the
tomatoes in the dish and tuck the whole,
unpeeled garlic cloves evenly in among
the tomatoes.

2 Brush the tomatoes with the oil, add
the bay leaves and sprinkle black pepper
over the top. Bake for about 45 minutes,
or until the tomatoes have softened and
are sizzling in the dish. Season with salt
and more black pepper, if needed.
Garnish with oregano leaves and serve.

SLOW-COOKED SPICED ONIONS

Onions marinated and baked in a spicy sauce are delicious with grilled or roasted meats.
Choose a good, extra virgin olive oil for a rich, peppery flavour.

SERVES 4

675g/1½lb red or Spanish onions
90ml/6 tbsp olive or sunflower oil or a
    mixture of both
pinch of saffron threads
2.5ml/½ tsp ground ginger
5ml/1 tsp ground black pepper
5ml/1 tsp ground cinnamon
15ml/1 tbsp sugar

1 Slice the onions very thinly and place them in a shallow dish. Blend together the olive and/or sunflower oil, saffron, ground ginger, black pepper, cinnamon and sugar, and pour over the onions. Stir gently to mix, then set the onions aside for about 2 hours.

2 Preheat the oven to 160°C/325°F/Gas 3 and pour the onions and the marinade into a casserole or ovenproof dish.

COOK'S TIP
Onions grown in warmer climates are milder than those from cooler regions. Consequently Spanish onions have a mild, sweet flavour. Their skins are a rich golden colour and they are one of the largest varieties available.

3 Fold a large piece of foil into three and place over the top of the casserole or ovenproof dish, securing it with a lid.

4 Cook in the oven for 45 minutes, or until the onions are very soft, then increase the oven temperature to 200°C/400°F/Gas 6. Remove the lid and foil and cook for a further 5–10 minutes, or until the onions are lightly glazed. Serve immediately.

COOK'S TIP
When slicing onions, chop off the neck and just a little of the base to help the onion stay together. Score a line down the side of the onion and peel away the outer skin and first layer of flesh.

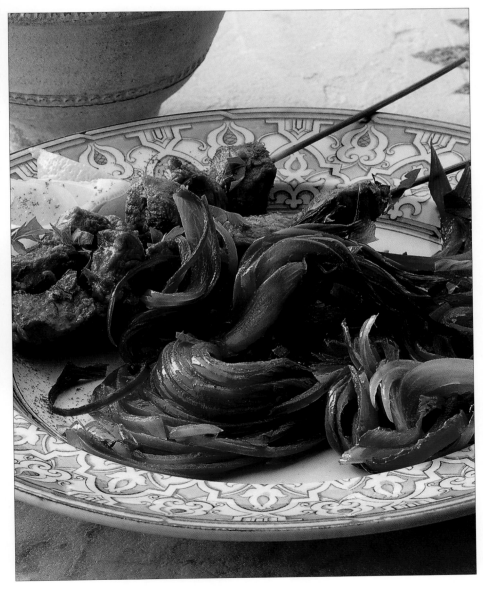

COURGETTES in TOMATO SAUCE

This rich-flavoured Mediterranean dish can be served hot or cold, either as a side dish or as part of a tapas meal. Cut the courgettes into fairly thick slices, so that they retain their texture and stay slightly crunchy.

SERVES 4

15ml/1 tbsp olive oil
1 onion, chopped
1 garlic clove, chopped
4 courgettes (zucchini), thickly sliced
400g/14oz can chopped tomatoes,
    drained
2 tomatoes, peeled, seeded and chopped
5ml/1 tsp vegetable bouillon powder
15ml/1 tbsp tomato purée (paste)
salt and ground black pepper

VARIATION
Add 1 or 2 sliced and seeded red, green or yellow (bell) peppers with the courgettes in step 1.

1 Heat the olive oil in a heavy pan, add the chopped onion and garlic and sauté for about 5 minutes, or until the onion is softened, stirring occasionally. Add the thickly sliced courgettes and cook for a further 5 minutes.

2 Add the canned and fresh tomatoes, bouillon powder and tomato purée. Stir well, then simmer for 10–15 minutes until the sauce is thickened and the courgettes are just tender. Season to taste and serve.

BAKED FENNEL with a CRUMB CRUST

The delicate aniseed flavour of baked fennel makes it a very good accompaniment to all kinds of dishes, from pasta and risotto to roast chicken.

SERVES 4

3 fennel bulbs, cut lengthwise
    into quarters
30ml/2 tbsp olive oil
1 garlic clove, chopped
50g/2oz/1 cup day-old wholemeal
    (whole-wheat) breadcrumbs
30ml/2 tbsp chopped fresh flat
    leaf parsley
salt and ground black pepper
a few fronds of fennel leaves, to
    garnish (optional)

COOK'S TIPS
• When buying fennel, look for compact, unblemished white-green bulbs. The leaves should look fresh and green. Tougher specimens will have bulbs that spread at the top.
• Fennel has a distinctive liquorice flavour, which particularly complements fish dishes. All parts of the plant are edible including the bulb, the celery-like stalks and the feathery leaves.

1 Cook the fennel in a pan of boiling salted water for 10 minutes. Preheat the oven to 190°C/375°F/Gas 5.

2 Drain the fennel and place in a large earthenware baking dish or baking tray, then brush with half of the olive oil.

VARIATION
To make a cheese-topped version, add 60ml/4 tbsp finely grated strong-flavoured cheese, such as mature (sharp) Cheddar, Red Leicester or Parmesan, to the breadcrumb mixture in step 3.

3 In a small bowl, mix together the chopped garlic, wholemeal breadcrumbs and chopped fresh flat leaf parsley, then stir in the rest of the olive oil. Sprinkle the mixture evenly over the fennel, then season well with salt and pepper.

4 Bake the fennel for about 30 minutes, or until it is tender and the breadcrumb topping is crisp and golden brown. Serve the baked fennel hot, garnished with a few fronds of fennel leaves, if you like.

ROOT VEGETABLE GRATIN with INDIAN SPICES

Subtly spiced with curry powder, turmeric, coriander and mild chilli powder, this rich gratin is substantial enough to serve on its own for lunch or supper. It also makes a good accompaniment to a vegetable or bean curry.

2 Preheat the oven to 180°C/350°F/ Gas 4. Heat half the butter in a heavy pan, add the curry powder, ground turmeric and coriander and half the chilli powder. Cook for 2 minutes, then leave to cool slightly. Drain the vegetables, then pat them dry with kitchen paper. Place in a bowl, add the spice mixture and the shallots and mix well.

3 Arrange the vegetables in a shallow baking dish, seasoning well with salt and pepper between the layers. Mix together the cream and milk, pour the mixture over the vegetables, then sprinkle the remaining chilli powder on top.

4 Cover the dish with baking parchment and bake for 45 minutes. Remove the baking parchment, dot the vegetables with the remaining butter and bake for a further 50 minutes, or until the top is golden brown. Serve the gratin garnished with chopped parsley.

SERVES 4

2 large potatoes, about 450g/1lb
   total weight
2 sweet potatoes, about 275g/10oz
   total weight
175g/6oz celeriac
15ml/1 tbsp unsalted (sweet) butter
5ml/1 tsp curry powder
5ml/1 tsp ground turmeric
2.5ml/½ tsp ground coriander
5ml/1 tsp mild chilli powder
3 shallots, chopped
150ml/¼ pint/⅔ cup single (light) cream
150ml/¼ pint/⅔ cup milk
salt and ground black pepper
chopped fresh flat leaf parsley, to garnish

1 Cut the potatoes, sweet potatoes and celeriac into thin, even slices using a sharp knife or the slicing attachment on a food processor. Immediately place the vegetables in a bowl of cold water to prevent them from discolouring.

COOK'S TIP
The cream adds a delicious richness to this gratin; use semi-skimmed (low-fat) milk, if you prefer a lighter meal.

ROASTED SWEET POTATOES, ONIONS and BEETROOT in COCONUT and GINGER PASTE

Sweet potatoes and beetroot take on a wonderful sweetness when roasted, and are delicious with savoury onions and aromatic coconut, ginger and garlic paste.

SERVES 4

30ml/2 tbsp groundnut (peanut) or mild
   olive oil
450g/1lb sweet potatoes, peeled and cut
   into thick strips or chunks
4 beetroot (beets), cooked, peeled and cut
   into wedges
450g/1lb small onions, halved
5ml/1 tsp coriander seeds, lightly crushed
3–4 small whole fresh red chillies
salt and ground black pepper
chopped fresh coriander (cilantro), to garnish

For the paste
2 large garlic cloves, chopped
1–2 green chillies, seeded and chopped
15ml/1 tbsp chopped fresh root ginger
45ml/3 tbsp chopped fresh coriander (cilantro)
75ml/5 tbsp coconut milk
30ml/2 tbsp groundnut (peanut) or mild
   olive oil
grated rind of ½ lime
2.5ml/½ tsp soft light brown sugar

1 To make the paste, process the garlic, chillies, ginger, coriander and coconut milk in a food processor or blender.

2 Tip the spicy paste into a small bowl and beat in the oil, grated lime rind and light brown sugar. Preheat the oven to 200°C/400°F/Gas 6.

3 Heat the oil in a large roasting pan in the oven for 5 minutes. Add the sweet potatoes, beetroot, onions and coriander seeds, tossing them in the hot oil. Roast the vegetables for 10 minutes.

4 Stir in the spicy paste and the whole red chillies. Season the vegetables well with salt and pepper, and shake the roasting pan to toss the vegetables and coat them thoroughly with the paste.

5 Return the vegetables to the oven and cook for a further 25–35 minutes, or until both the sweet potatoes and onions are fully cooked and tender. During cooking, stir the mixture two or three times with a wooden spoon to prevent the coconut and ginger paste from sticking to the roasting pan. Serve the vegetables immediately, sprinkled with a little chopped fresh coriander.

COOK'S TIP
Try to buy orange-fleshed sweet potatoes for this dish – they not only look more attractive than white-fleshed ones in this dish, they are also more nutritious.

CHEESE-TOPPED ROAST BABY VEGETABLES

A simple way of serving baby vegetables that really brings out their flavour.

SERVES 4

1kg/2¼lb mixed baby vegetables, such as
   aubergines (eggplant), onions or
   shallots, courgettes (zucchini), corn
   cobs and mushrooms
1 red (bell) pepper, seeded and cut into
   large pieces
1–2 garlic cloves, finely chopped
15–30ml/1–2 tbsp olive oil
30ml/2 tbsp chopped fresh mixed herbs
225g/8oz cherry tomatoes
115g/4oz/1 cup coarsely grated
   mozzarella cheese
salt and ground black pepper
black olives, to serve (optional)

1 Preheat the oven to 220°C/425°F/Gas 7.
Cut the vegetables in half lengthwise.

2 Place the halved baby vegetables and
pepper pieces in an ovenproof dish with
the finely chopped garlic and plenty of salt
and ground black pepper. Drizzle the oil
over and toss the vegetables to coat them.
Bake the vegetables for 20 minutes, or
until they are tinged brown at the edges,
stirring once during the cooking time.

3 Remove the ovenproof dish from the
oven and stir in the chopped fresh mixed
herbs. Sprinkle the cherry tomatoes over
the surface and top with the coarsely
grated mozzarella cheese. Return to the
oven and bake for 5–10 minutes more
until the cheese has melted and is
bubbling. Serve immediately with black
olives, if you like.

COOK'S TIP

This dish can also be made with a mixture
of regular-sized vegetables. Simply chop
them into bitesize pieces and continue
from Step 2.

VARIATION

Use 2–3 sprigs of fresh rosemary in place
of the chopped fresh mixed herbs.

BAKED SCALLOPED POTATOES with FETA CHEESE and OLIVES

Thinly sliced potatoes are cooked with Greek feta cheese and black and green olives and olive oil. This dish would also make a good light lunch served with a salad.

SERVES 4

4–6 large, unpeeled potatoes, total weight about 900g/2lb
150ml/¼ pint/⅔ cup extra virgin olive oil
leaves from a sprig of rosemary
275g/10oz/2½ cups feta cheese, coarsely crumbled
115g/4oz/1 cup pitted mixed black and green olives
300ml/½ pint/1¼ cups hot vegetable stock
salt and ground black pepper

1 Preheat the oven to 200°C/400°F/ Gas 6. Bring a large pan of salted water to the boil and cook the potatoes, still in their skins, for 15 minutes until only just tender.

2 Drain the potatoes and set them aside until they are cool enough to handle. Carefully remove the peel from the potatoes using a small sharp knife and then cut them into thin slices.

3 Brush the base and sides of a 1.5 litre/ 2½ pint/6¼ cup rectangular ovenproof dish with some of the olive oil.

COOK'S TIP
Cooking the potatoes with their skins on not only helps to preserve their vitamin content, but will also ensure that the potatoes cook more evenly. If you prefer, peel them before they are cooked.

4 Arrange half the potatoes in the dish in an even layer. Top with half of the rosemary, cheese and olives and season with salt and pepper. Arrange the rest of the potatoes in an even layer on top.

5 Add the remaining rosemary leaves, crumbled cheese and olives, and drizzle with the remaining olive oil. Pour the hot vegetable stock over the top and season the top layer with salt and plenty of ground black pepper.

6 Bake for 35 minutes, covering the dish loosely with foil after about 20 minutes to prevent the potatoes from getting too brown. Serve hot, straight from the dish.

VARIATION
Thinly sliced sun-dried tomatoes would make a delicious addition.

POTATO GRATIN

Potatoes, layered with mustard butter and baked until golden, are perfect to serve with a green salad, or as an accompaniment to a vegetable or nut roast.

SERVES 4

4 large potatoes, about 900g/2lb
   total weight
30ml/2 tbsp butter
15ml/1 tbsp olive oil
2 large garlic cloves, crushed
30ml/2 tbsp Dijon mustard
15ml/1 tbsp lemon juice
15ml/1 tbsp fresh thyme leaves, plus
   extra to garnish
50ml/2fl oz/¼ cup vegetable stock
salt and ground black pepper

1 Thinly slice the potatoes using a knife, mandolin or a slicing attachment on a food processor. Place the potato slices in a bowl of cold water to prevent them from discolouring.

2 Preheat the oven to 200°C/400°F/ Gas 6. Heat the butter and oil in a deep, flameproof frying pan. Add the garlic and cook gently for 2–3 minutes until light golden, stirring constantly. Stir in the mustard, lemon juice and thyme. Remove from the heat and pour the mixture into a jug (pitcher).

3 Drain the potatoes and pat dry with kitchen paper. Place a layer of potatoes in the frying pan, season and pour over one-third of the butter mixture. Arrange another layer of potatoes on top, pour over half of the remaining butter mixture and season. Arrange a final layer of potatoes on top, pour over the remainder of butter mixture and the stock. Season and sprinkle with the reserved thyme.

4 Cover the potatoes with baking parchment and bake for 1 hour, then remove the paper, return to the oven and cook for 15 minutes, or until golden.

VARIATION
Any root vegetables can be used: try sweet potatoes, parsnips or turnips.

POTATOES BAKED with FENNEL, ONIONS, GARLIC and SAFFRON

Potatoes, fennel and onions flavoured with garlic, saffron and spices make a sophisticated and attractive accompaniment to fish, chicken or egg-based main-course dishes.

SERVES 4–6

500g/1¼lb small waxy potatoes, cut into
    chunks or wedges
good pinch of saffron threads
    (12–15 threads)
1 head of garlic, separated into
    individual cloves
12 small red or yellow onions, peeled
    but left whole
3 fennel bulbs, cut into wedges, feathery
    tops reserved for garnish (optional)
4–6 fresh bay leaves
6–9 fresh thyme sprigs
175ml/6fl oz/¾ cup fish, chicken or
    vegetable stock
30ml/2 tbsp sherry or
    balsamic vinegar
2.5ml/½ tsp sugar
5ml/1 tsp fennel seeds, lightly crushed
2.5ml/½ tsp paprika
45ml/3 tbsp olive oil
salt and ground black pepper

1 Boil the potato chunks or wedges in a pan of boiling salted water for 8–10 minutes. Drain. Preheat the oven to 190°C/375°F/Gas 5. Soak the saffron threads in 30ml/2 tbsp warm water for 10 minutes.

2 Peel and finely chop two of the garlic cloves and set aside. Place the potato chunks or wedges, whole red or yellow onions, remaining unpeeled garlic cloves, fennel wedges, fresh bay leaves and fresh thyme sprigs in a large roasting pan or dish. Mix together the stock and the saffron and its soaking liquid in a jug (pitcher) or measuring cup.

3 Add the vinegar and sugar to the stock mixture, then pour the liquid over the vegetables. Stir in the fennel seeds, paprika, chopped garlic and oil, and season with salt and pepper.

4 Cook the vegetables in the oven for 1–1¼ hours, stirring occasionally, until they are just tender. Chop the reserved fennel tops, if using, and sprinkle them over the vegetables to garnish. Season the vegetables with more salt and pepper and serve immediately.

COOK'S TIP
Sherry vinegar has a rich, mellow flavour and it makes a good addition to a variety of sauces and dressings. It can be used simply to add extra piquancy to a dish. Try sprinkling a little over oven-roasted vegetables or add a teaspoon or two to soups, sauces or stews.

ROASTED POTATOES with GARLIC and RED ONIONS

These mouthwatering potatoes are a fine accompaniment to just about anything. The key is to use small firm potatoes; the smaller they are cut, the quicker they will cook.

SERVES 4

675g/1½lb small firm potatoes
25g/1oz/2 tbsp butter
30ml/2 tbsp olive oil
2 large or 4 small red onions, cut
   into wedges
8 garlic cloves, unpeeled
30ml/2 tbsp chopped fresh rosemary or
   10ml/2 tsp dried
salt and ground black pepper

COOK'S TIP
Choose waxy or new potatoes that will hold their shape for this dish. You can peel them, or simply scrub them well and leave the skins on.

1 Preheat the oven to 230°C/450°F/ Gas 8. Peel and quarter the potatoes, rinse them and pat dry on kitchen paper.

2 Put the butter and oil in a roasting pan and heat in the oven. When the butter has melted and is foaming, add the potatoes, onion wedges and garlic cloves to the roasting pan.

3 Sprinkle over the rosemary, toss well then spread out the vegetables.

4 Place the pan in the oven and roast for about 25 minutes until the potatoes are golden and tender when tested with a fork. Shake the pan from time to time to redistribute the vegetables. When cooked, season with salt and pepper.

SAFFRON RICE with ONION and CARDAMOM

This delightfully fragrant, buttery pilaff is wonderful with both Indian and Middle-eastern dishes, especially ones featuring fish, shellfish, chicken or lamb.

2 Toast the saffron threads in a dry, heavy frying pan over a low heat for about 2 minutes, then place in a small bowl and add 30ml/2 tbsp warm water. Leave to soak for 10–15 minutes.

3 Melt the butter in the pan, then cook the onion with the cardamom pods very gently for 8–10 minutes, until soft and buttery yellow.

4 Add the drained rice to the pan and stir to coat the grains in the butter. Add the salt and bay leaves, then stir in the stock or water and saffron with its liquid. Bring the rice to the boil, stir, then reduce the heat to very low and cover tightly. Cook the rice for 10–12 minutes, until it has absorbed all the liquid.

SERVES 4

350g/12oz/1¾ cups basmati rice
good pinch of saffron threads (about 15 threads)
25g/1oz/2 tbsp butter
1 onion, finely chopped
6 green cardamom pods, lightly crushed
5ml/1 tsp salt
2–3 fresh bay leaves
600ml/1 pint/2½ cups well-flavoured chicken or vegetable stock or water

1 Put the rice into a sieve and rinse well under cold running water. Tip it into a bowl, add cold water to cover and set aside to soak for 30–40 minutes. Drain in the sieve.

COOK'S TIP

After boiling, when all the liquid has been absorbed, basmati rice is set aside to finish cooking in its own heat and become tender. Wedging a folded dishtowel under the pan lid ensures the heat is not lost and the steam is absorbed.

5 Lay a clean, folded dishtowel over the pan under the lid and press on the lid to wedge it firmly in place. Leave the rice to stand for 10–15 minutes to continue cooking in its own heat.

6 Fluff up the grains of cooked rice with a fork. Tip it into a warmed serving dish and serve immediately as an accompaniment to a spicy main course.

BASMATI RICE with VEGETABLES

Serve this tasty dish with roast chicken, grilled lamb cutlets or pan-fried fish. Add the vegetables near the end of cooking so that they remain crisp.

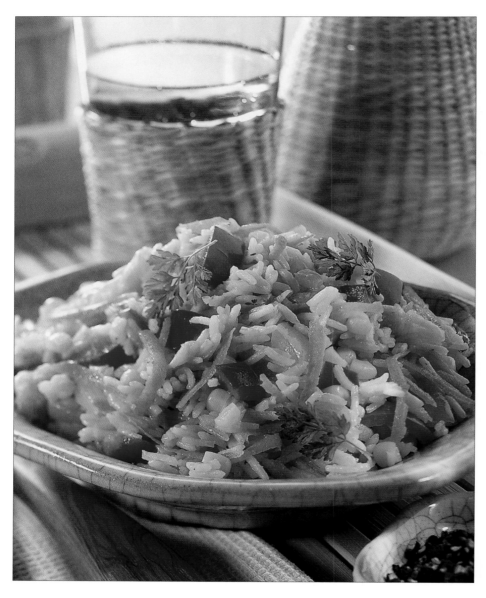

SERVES 4

350g/12oz/1¾ cups basmati rice
45ml/3 tbsp vegetable oil
1 onion, chopped
2 garlic cloves, crushed
750ml/1¼ pints/3 cups water or
  vegetable stock
115g/4oz/⅔ cup fresh or drained canned
  corn kernels
1 red or green (bell) pepper, seeded
  and chopped
1 large carrot, grated
fresh chervil sprigs, to garnish

2 Heat the oil in a large pan and fry the onion for a few minutes over a medium heat until it starts to soften.

3 Add the rice to the pan and fry for about 10 minutes, stirring constantly to prevent the rice sticking to the base of the pan. Stir in the crushed garlic.

4 Pour in the water or stock and stir well. Bring to the boil, then lower the heat. Cover and simmer for 10 minutes.

1 Rinse the rice in a sieve under cold water, then leave to drain thoroughly for about 15 minutes.

5 Sprinkle the corn over the rice, spread the chopped pepper on top and sprinkle over the grated carrot. Cover tightly and steam over a low heat until the rice is tender, then mix with a fork. Pile on to a serving plate and garnish with chervil.

GARLIC CHIVE RICE with MUSHROOMS

Rice is readily infused with the pungent aroma and taste of garlic chives, creating a dish with an excellent flavour. Serve with vegetarian dishes, fish or chicken.

SERVES 4

60ml/4 tbsp groundnut (peanut) oil
250g/9oz mixed mushrooms,
    thickly sliced
25g/1oz garlic chives, chopped
350g/12oz/1¾ cups long grain rice
1 small onion, finely chopped
2 green chillies, seeded and finely chopped
15g/½oz fresh coriander (cilantro)
600ml/1 pint/2½ cups vegetable or
    mushroom stock
5ml/1 tsp salt
50g/2oz toasted cashew nuts
ground black pepper

5 Add the rice to the onions and fry over a low heat, stirring frequently, for 4–5 minutes until the onion is softened. Pour in the stock mixture, then stir in the salt and plenty of black pepper.

6 Bring to the boil, stir and reduce the heat to very low. Cover tightly and cook for 15–20 minutes, until the rice has absorbed all the liquid.Lay a clean, folded dishtowel over the pan under the lid and press on the lid to wedge it firmly in place. Leave to stand in a warm place for 10 minutes, allowing the towel to absorb the steam while the rice becomes completely tender.

7 Add the cooked mushroom and chive mixture to the rice and mix well. Stir in the chopped fresh coriander leaves, then adjust the seasoning. Serve immediately, sprinkled with the toasted cashew nuts.

1 Heat half the oil in a large frying pan and cook the thickly sliced mushrooms for 5–6 minutes, stirring occasionally, until they are tender and browned.

2 Add half of the garlic chives to the pan and cook for 1–2 minutes. Remove from the pan using a slotted spoon and set aside. Wash and drain the rice.

3 Add the remaining oil to the frying pan, add the chopped onion and chillies and cook over a gentle heat, stirring occasionally, for 10–12 minutes, until the onions have softened.

4 Set half the remaining garlic chives aside. Cut the stalks off the coriander and set the leaves aside. Purée the remaining chives and the coriander stalks with the stock in a food processor or blender.

COOK'S TIP
You'll find garlic chives in Asian and Thai food stores.

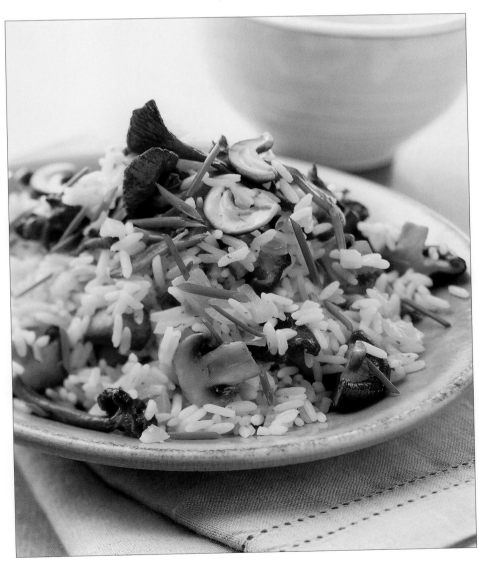

RICE with DILL and BROAD BEANS

This is a favourite rice dish in Iran. The combination of broad beans, plenty of fresh dill and warm spices works very well, and the saffron rice adds a splash of bright colour.

SERVES 4

275g/10oz/1½ cups basmati rice,
    soaked in cold water and drained
750ml/1¼ pints/3 cups water
40g/1½oz/3 tbsp butter
175g/6oz/1½ cups frozen baby broad (fava)
    beans, thawed and peeled
90ml/6 tbsp finely chopped fresh dill, plus
    fresh dill sprigs to garnish
5ml/1 tsp ground cinnamon
5ml/1 tsp ground cumin
2–3 saffron threads, soaked in
    15ml/1 tbsp boiling water
salt

1 Tip the rice into a large pan with the water. Add a little salt. Bring to the boil, then simmer very gently for 5 minutes. Drain, rinse in warm water and drain again.

2 Melt the butter in the rinsed-out pan. Pour two-thirds of the melted butter into a bowl and set aside. Spoon enough rice into the pan to cover the base. Add one-quarter of the beans and a little dill.

3 Spread over another layer of rice, then a layer of beans and dill. Repeat the layers until all the beans and dill have been used, ending with a layer of rice. Cook over a gentle heat for 8 minutes until nearly tender.

4 Pour the reserved melted butter evenly over the rice, then sprinkle the ground cinnamon and cumin over the top. Cover the pan with a clean dishtowel or cloth and a tight-fitting lid, lifting the corners of the towel or cloth back over the lid. Cook over a low heat for 25–30 minutes.

5 Spoon about 45ml/3 tbsp of the cooked rice into the bowl of saffron water and then mix the rice and liquid together. Spoon the remaining rice mixture on to a large serving plate and spoon the saffron rice on one side to garnish. Serve immediately, decorated with fresh sprigs of dill.

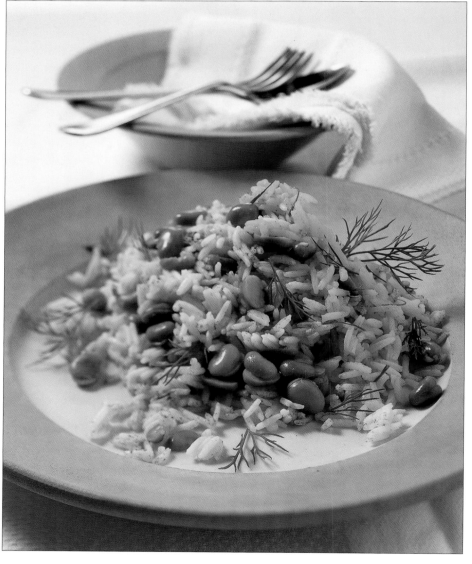

LENTIL DHAL with ROASTED GARLIC and WHOLE SPICES

This spicy lentil dhal makes a sustaining and comforting meal when served with rice or Indian breads and any dry-spiced dish, particularly a cauliflower or potato dish. It's a bit of a cheat to have in a one-pot cookbook, since there's a spicy garnish that needs to be cooked separately.

SERVES 4–6

40g/1½oz/3 tbsp butter or ghee
1 onion, chopped
2 green chillies, seeded and chopped
15ml/1 tbsp chopped fresh root ginger
225g/8oz/1 cup yellow or red lentils
900ml/1½ pints/3¾ cups water
45ml/3 tbsp roasted garlic purée
5ml/1 tsp ground cumin
5ml/1 tsp ground coriander
200g/7oz tomatoes, peeled and diced
a little lemon juice
salt and ground black pepper
30–45ml/2–3 tbsp coriander (cilantro)
    sprigs, to garnish

For the spicy garnish
30ml/2 tbsp groundnut (peanut) oil
4–5 shallots, sliced
2 garlic cloves, thinly sliced
15g/½oz/1 tbsp butter or ghee
5ml/1 tsp cumin seeds
5ml/1 tsp mustard seeds
3–4 small dried red chillies
8–10 fresh curry leaves

1 First begin the spicy garnish. Heat the oil in a large, heavy pan. Add the shallots and fry them over a medium heat, stirring occasionally, until they are crisp and browned. Add the garlic and cook, stirring frequently, for a moment or two until the garlic colours slightly. Use a slotted spoon to remove the mixture from the pan and set aside.

COOK'S TIP
Ghee is a type of clarified butter that has had all the milk solids removed by heating – it was originally made to extend the keeping qualities of butter in India. It is the main cooking fat used in Indian cooking. Because the milk solids have been removed, ghee has a high smoking point and can therefore be cooked at higher temperatures than ordinary butter. Look for it in Indian and Asian stores.

2 To make the dhal, Melt the butter or ghee in the pan and cook the onion, green chillies and ginger for 10 minutes until golden.

3 Stir in the lentils and water, then bring to the boil, reduce the heat and part-cover the pan. Simmer, stirring occasionally, for 50–60 minutes until similar to a very thick soup.

4 Stir in the roasted garlic purée, ground cumin and ground coriander, then season with salt and pepper to taste. Cook for a further 10–15 minutes, uncovered, stirring frequently.

5 Stir in the tomatoes and adjust the seasoning, adding lemon juice to taste.

6 To finish the spicy garnish: melt the butter or ghee in a frying pan. Add the cumin and mustard seeds and fry until the mustard seeds pop. Stir in the chillies, curry leaves and half the shallot mixture, then immediately swirl the mixture into the cooked dhal. Garnish with coriander, remaining shallot mixture and serve.

INDEX

A

apples: grouse with orchard fruit stuffing, 66
noisettes of pork with creamy Calvados and apple sauce, 37
pot-roast loin of pork with apple, 36
aubergines: Moroccan fish tagine, 99
ratatouille, 116

B

bacon: braised pheasants with wild mushrooms, chestnuts and, 67
lamb's liver casserole, 50
baking dishes, 8–9
basmati rice and nut pilaff, 122
basmati rice with vegetables, 154
beans: black bean chilli con carne, 59
cassoulet, 84
Catalan potato and broad bean soup, 22
Jamaican black bean pot, 118
pancetta and broad bean risotto, 40
pork cooked in cider, 34
rice with dill and, 156
roast lamb with green peppercorns and, 48
beef: beef carbonade, 52
black bean chilli con carne, 59
boeuf bourguignon, 53
citrus beef curry, 56
fillet of beef Stroganoff, 54
pot-roast beef with Guinness, 55
boeuf bourguignon, 53
bouillabaisse, 18
braising meat, 10
Brazilian pork and rice casserole, 38
brill in red wine sauce, 93
broccoli, anchovy and pasta soup, 16
bruschetta, chicken liver and onion, 58
buckwheat noodles with cabbage, potatoes and cheese, 124

C

cabbage: buckwheat noodles with potatoes, cheese and, 124
calf's liver with slow-cooked onions, Marsala and sage, 58
carrots, braised with leeks, 136
casseroles and stews, 10–11
beef carbonade, 52
boeuf bourguignon, 53
braised lamb with apricots and herb dumplings, 47
braised pheasant with wild mushrooms, chestnuts and bacon, 67
braised shoulder of lamb with pearl barley and baby vegetables, 46
Brazilian pork and rice casserole, 38
cassoulet, 84
chicken casserole with winter vegetables, 70
chicken with chickpeas and almonds, 76
chicken with tomatoes and honey, 76
coq au vin, 71
fish with fregola, 97
grouse with orchard fruit stuffing, 66
hunter's chicken, 72
Irish stew, 44
Italian fish stew, 100
Jamaican black bean pot, 118
marinated pigeon in red wine, 65
Mediterranean duck with harissa and saffron, 87
octopus and red wine stew, 103
ostrich stew with sweet potatoes and chickpeas, 64
pork cooked in cider with parsley dumplings, 34
ratatouille, 116
Seville chicken, 73
spicy venison casserole, 61
see also tagines
cassoulet, 84
Catalan potato and broad bean soup, 22
cauliflower with tomatoes and cumin, 140
cheese: baked scalloped potatoes with feta cheese and olives, 149
buckwheat noodles with cabbage, potatoes and, 124
cheese-topped roast baby vegetables, 148
fettucine with butter and Parmesan, 124
pan haggerty, 115

pasta shells with tomatoes and ricotta, 131
pasta twists with pesto, 126
pasta with cream and, 127
spaghetti with black pepper and, 128
truffade, 112
chicken: chicken and leek soup, 28
chicken and prawn jambalaya, 82
chicken baked with shallots, garlic and fennel, 74
chicken biriani, 81
chicken casserole with winter vegetables, 70
chicken liver and onion bruschetta, 58
chicken piri-piri, 80
chicken with chickpeas and almonds, 76
chicken with forty cloves of garlic, 75
chicken with tomatoes and honey, 76
cooking techniques, 11
coq au vin, 71
hunter's chicken, 72
oven-roasted chicken with Mediterranean vegetables, 78
risotto with chicken, 83
Seville chicken, 73
chickpeas: chicken with almonds and, 76
ostrich stew with sweet potatoes and, 64
chow mein, pork, 33
chowder: clam, mushroom and potato, 25
seafood, 26
citrus beef curry, 56
clams: clam, mushroom and potato chowder, 25
mussels and clams with lemon grass and coconut cream, 104
seafood paella, 106
cod: cod and prawn green coconut curry, 102
fish plaki, 98
fish with fregola, 97

coq au vin, 71
courgettes in tomato sauce, 144
couscous: lamb and pumpkin couscous, 45
vegetable couscous with saffron and harissa, 123
curries: citrus beef curry, 56
cod and prawn green coconut curry, 102
spiced lamb with tomatoes and peppers, 43
tofu and vegetable Thai curry, 120
vegetable korma, 119

D

devilled kidneys on brioche croûtes, 51
duck: cassoulet, 84
Mediterranean duck with harissa and saffron, 87
stir-fried crispy duck, 86
dumplings: braised lamb with apricots and herb dumplings, 47
pork cooked in cider with parsley dumplings, 34

E

eggplant see aubergines
equipment, 8–9

F

fennel: baked fennel with a crumb crust, 144
chicken baked with shallots, garlic and, 74
potatoes baked with onions, garlic, saffron and, 151
fettucine with butter and Parmesan, 124
fish: bouillabaisse, 18
fish plaki, 98
fish stew with lemon grass, 101
fish with fregola, 97
fish with spinach and lime, 95
Goan fish casserole, 180
Italian fish stew, 100
Mediterranean leek and fish soup with tomatoes, 19
Moroccan fish tagine, 99
see also cod, hake, monkfish, tuna etc
free-standing cooking pots, 9
frittata: leek, red pepper and spinach, 114
tuna, 91

G

gammon: chicken and prawn
jambalaya, 82
garlic chive rice with
mushrooms, 155
gingered seafood stir-fry, 105
gratins: Jansson's temptation, 92
potato gratin, 150
root vegetable gratin with
Indian spices, 146
grouse with orchard fruit
stuffing, 66

H

ham: pan-fried ham and
vegetables with eggs, 41
hunter's chicken, 72

I

Irish stew, 44
Italian farmhouse soup, 15
Italian fish stew, 100

J

Jamaican black bean pot, 118
jambalaya, 82
Jansson's temptation, 92

K

kidneys: devilled kidneys on
brioche croûtes, 51

L

lamb: braised lamb with
apricots and herb
dumplings, 47
braised shoulder of lamb
with pearl barley and
baby vegetables, 46
Irish stew, 44
lamb and pumpkin
couscous, 45
Middle-Eastern roast lamb
and potatoes, 49
minted lamb stir-fry, 42
Moroccan spiced lamb
soup, 21
roast lamb with beans and
green peppercorns, 48
spiced lamb with tomatoes
and peppers, 43

leeks: braised baby leeks in red
wine, 137
braised carrots with, 136
braised leeks in tarragon
cream, 136
chicken and leek soup, 28
frittata with red pepper,
spinach and, 114
Mediterranean leek and fish
soup with tomatoes, 19
lentils: lentil and pasta soup, 14
lentil dhal with roasted garlic
and whole spices, 157
Mediterranean sausage and
pesto soup, 20
lettuce: braised lettuce and peas
with mint, 138
linguine with rocket, 132
liver: calf's liver with
slow-cooked onions,
Marsala and sage, 58
chicken liver and onion
bruschetta, 58
lamb's liver and bacon
casserole, 50

M

meat, cooking, 10–11
Mediterranean duck with
harissa and saffron, 87
Mediterranean leek and fish
soup with tomatoes, 19
Mediterranean sausage and
pesto soup, 20
Mediterranean vegetables baked
in golden batter, 111
Middle-Eastern roast lamb and
potatoes, 49
monkfish: baked monkfish with
potatoes and garlic, 94
Italian fish stew, 100
Moroccan fish tagine, 99
Moroccan spiced lamb soup, 21
mushrooms: boeuf
bourguignon, 53
braised pheasant with wild
mushrooms, chestnuts and
bacon, 67
clam, mushroom and potato
chowder, 25
fillet of beef Stroganoff, 54
garlic chive rice with, 155
hunter's chicken, 72
venison sausages with red
wine gravy, 62
mussels: Italian fish stew, 100
mussels and clams with
lemon grass and coconut
cream, 104
seafood paella, 106

N

noodles: buckwheat noodles
with cabbage, potatoes and
cheese, 124
pork chow mein, 33

O

octopus and red wine stew, 103
okra and tomato tagine, 117
onions: calf's liver with
slow-cooked onions,
Marsala and sage, 58
pan haggerty, 115
potatoes baked with fennel,
garlic, saffron and, 151
roasted potatoes with garlic
and, 152
roasted sweet potatoes,
beetroot and onions in
a coconut and ginger
paste, 147
saffron rice with cardamom
and, 153
slow-cooked spiced onions, 143
truffade, 112
osso bucco with risotto
milanese, 60
ostrich stew with sweet
potatoes and chickpeas, 64
oven-roasted chicken with
Mediterranean vegetables, 78

P

paella: seafood paella, 106
pan frying, 11
pan haggerty, 115
pancetta and broad bean
risotto, 40
pasta: fish with fregola, 97
pasta shells with tomatoes
and ricotta, 131
pasta squares and peas in
broth, 16
pasta twists with pesto, 126
pasta with cheese and
cream, 127
see also linguine, spaghetti etc
penne with cream and smoked
salmon, 90
pheasant: braised pheasant
with wild mushrooms,
chestnuts and bacon, 67
pigeon: marinated pigeon in red
wine, 65
pork: Brazilian pork and rice
casserole, 38

noisettes of pork with creamy
Calvados and apple sauce, 37
pork chow mein, 33
pork cooked in cider with
parsley dumplings, 34
pot-roast loin of pork with
apple, 36
sweet-and-sour pork
stir-fry, 32
pot-roasting, 10
pot-roasts: chicken with forty
cloves of garlic, 75
pot-roast beef with
Guinness, 55
pot-roast loin of pork with
apple, 36
roast lamb with beans and
green peppercorns, 48
potatoes: baked monkfish with
garlic and, 94
baked scalloped, with feta
cheese and olives, 149
baked sea bream with
tomatoes, 96
buckwheat noodles with
cabbage, cheese and, 124
Catalan potato and broad
bean soup, 22
fish with spinach and lime, 95

Irish stew, 44
Jansson's temptation, 92
Middle-Eastern roast lamb
and, 49
new potatoes and
vegetables baked
Turkish-style, 110
pan haggerty, 115
potato gratin, 150
potatoes baked with
fennel, onions, garlic
and saffron, 151
potatoes baked with
tomatoes, 112
roasted potatoes with garlic
and red onions, 152
root vegetable gratin with
Indian spices, 146
Spanish potato and garlic
soup, 22
truffade, 112

pots and pans, 8–9
prawns: chicken and prawn
    jambalaya, 82
    coconut and seafood soup, 29
    cod and prawn green
        coconut curry, 102
    seafood paella, 106
pumpkin and lamb couscous, 45

R
rabbit with red wine and
    prunes, 63
ratatouille, 116
red mullet: fish with
    fregola, 97
red snapper: fish with
    fregola, 97
rice: basmati rice and nut
    pilaff, 122
    basmati rice with
        vegetables, 154
    Brazilian pork and rice
        casserole, 38
    chicken and prawn
        jambalaya, 82
    chicken biriani, 81
    chicken piri-piri, 80
    garlic chive rice with
        mushrooms, 155
    rice with dill and broad
        beans, 156
    saffron rice with onion
        and cardamom, 153
    seafood paella, 106
    Seville chicken, 73
risotto: pancetta and broad
    bean risotto, 40
    risotto milanese, 60
    risotto with chicken, 83
    seafood risotto, 107
roasts: Middle-Eastern roast
    lamb and potatoes, 49
    oven-roasted chicken
        with Mediterranean
        vegetables, 78
    see also pot-roasts
rocket: linguine with, 132
    spaghetti with rocket
        pesto, 130
root vegetable gratin with
    Indian spices, 146

S
saffron rice with onion and
    cardamom, 153
sausages: cassoulet, 84
    Mediterranean sausage and
        pesto soup, 20
    toad-in-the-hole, 39
    venison sausages with red
        wine gravy, 62
sea bream with
    tomatoes, 96
seafood: gingered seafood
    stir-fry, 105
    seafood chowder, 26
    seafood paella, 106
    seafood risotto, 107
Seville chicken, 73
shallots, chicken baked with
    garlic, fennel and, 74
shellfish: bouillabaisse, 18
shrimp see prawns
side dishes, 134–155
smoked salmon, penne with
    cream and, 90
soups, 12–29
    bouillabaisse, 18
    broccoli, anchovy and pasta
        soup, 16
    Catalan potato and broad
        bean soup, 22
    chicken and leek soup, 28
    clam, mushroom and potato
        chowder, 25
    coconut and seafood soup, 29
    corn and potato chowder, 24
    Italian farmhouse soup, 15
    lentil and pasta soup, 14
    Mediterranean leek and
        fish soup with
        tomatoes, 19
    Mediterranean sausage and
        pesto soup, 20
    Moroccan spiced lamb
        soup, 21
    pasta squares and peas in
        broth, 16
    seafood chowder, 26
    Spanish potato and garlic
        soup, 22
spaghetti: spaghetti with
    butter and herbs, 128
    spaghetti with cheese and
        black pepper, 128
    spaghetti with garlic and
        oil, 133
    spaghetti with rocket
        pesto, 130
Spanish potato and garlic
    soup, 22
spinach: fish with lime and, 95
    frittata with leek, red pepper
        and, 114
    roast lamb with beans and
        green peppercorns, 48
    spinach braised with sweet
        potatoes, 139

stews see casseroles and stews
stir-fries: gingered seafood
    stir-fry, 105
    minted lamb stir-fry, 42
    pork chow mein, 33
    stir-fried crispy duck, 86
    sweet-and-sour pork
        stir-fry, 32
stir-frying, 11
sweet-and-sour pork
    stir-fry, 32
sweet potatoes: ostrich stew
    with chickpeas and, 64
    roasted sweet potatoes,
        onions and beetroot in
        a coconut and ginger
        paste, 147
    root vegetable gratin with
        Indian spices, 146
    spinach braised with, 139

T
tagines: Moroccan fish, 99
    okra and tomato, 117
techniques, 10–11
toad-in-the-hole, 39
tofu and vegetable Thai
    curry, 120
tomatoes: baked sea bream
    with, 96
    cauliflower with cumin
        and, 140
    chicken and prawn
        jambalaya, 82
    chicken with honey and, 76
    courgettes in tomato
        sauce, 144
    Italian fish stew, 100
    octopus and red wine
        stew, 103
    okra and tomato
        tagine, 117
    pasta shells with tomatoes
        and ricotta, 131
    peeling, 10–11
    potatoes baked with
        tomatoes, 112
    roasted tomatoes, 63
    ratatouille, 116
    roasted tomatoes and
        garlic, 142
    spiced lamb with peppers
        and, 43
truffade, 112
tuna frittata, 91

V
veal: *osso bucco* with risotto
    milanese, 60
vegetables: basmati rice
    with, 154
    braised shoulder of lamb
        with pearl barley and
        baby vegetables, 46
    cheese-topped roast baby
        vegetables, 148

chicken casserole with
    winter vegetables, 70
Italian farmhouse
    soup, 15
Mediterranean vegetables
    baked in golden
    batter, 111
new potatoes and
    vegetables baked
    Turkish-style, 110
oven-roasted chicken
    with Mediterranean
    vegetables, 78
pan-fried ham and
    vegetables with
    eggs, 41
ratatouille, 116
roast vegetables with
    herbs and chilli
    sauce, 140
root vegetable gratin with
    Indian spices, 146
tofu and vegetable Thai
    curry, 120
vegetable couscous
    with saffron and
    harissa, 123
vegetable korma, 119
vegetarian dishes, 108–133
venison: spicy venison
    casserole, 61
    venison sausages with red
        wine gravy, 62

W
water chestnuts: stir-fried
    crispy duck, 86
wine: boeuf bourguignon, 53
    braised baby leeks in red
        wine, 137
    coq au vin, 71

marinated pigeon in red
    wine, 65
octopus and red wine
    stew, 103
rabbit with red wine and
    prunes, 63
venison sausages with red
    wine gravy, 62